To Pamela

May your path be
filled with joy, love,
beauty and peace.
always

Marilyn Lee

THAT WAS ERNEST

THAT WAS ERNEST

THE STORY OF ERNEST HOLMES

and

THE RELIGIOUS SCIENCE MOVEMENT

REGINALD C. ARMOR

as told to Robin Llast

Arthur Vergara, editor

DeVorss Publications
Marina del Rey, California

© 1999 Marilyn Leo

ISBN: 0-87516-712-8

Library of Congress Catalog Card Number 98-74806

The photographs in the special section after p. 74 appear courtesy of:
Mrs. Elsie Armor
Rev. Marilyn Leo (daughter)
The United Church of Religious Science

The illustrations appearing throughout the text portion appear
courtesy of The United Church of Religious Science
and the private collection of the editor.

DeVorss & Company, *Publishers*
Box 550
Marina del Rey CA 90294-0550

Printed in the United States of America

Pamela Elliott
Asilomar
August, 1999

DEDICATED

TO THE YOUTH OF THE WORLD

CONTENTS

A section of photographs appears following page 74.

A WORD FROM THE PUBLISHER

This personal and informal memoir is unique in the history of Religious Science, the Science of Mind, and New Thought. Written by the only person to have been beside Ernest Holmes on an almost daily basis from a time shortly after Holmes' move from Maine to California in 1912 until his death in 1960, it is important historically in three distinct ways.

First, it examines Ernest Holmes from up close, covering almost a half-century of day-to-day contact. Reginald Armor's life was dedicated to assisting Dr. Holmes as his close associate in developing his teaching and in organizing and administrating his work. In this he continued faithfully until his own passing in 1977.

Second, it is the account of one whose association with Dr. Holmes began as a twelve-year-old. This was in 1915, when Ernest Holmes was only twenty-eight, but already well on his way to becoming the master teacher he would be. Thus Reg Armor's adolescent and adult development was molded by an unvarying adherence to the principles and practice of the Science of Mind. He was truly the first pupil and ''graduate'' of this great transformative philosophy.

Third, in bearing unique witness to the history and development of the Religious Science movement, it testifies to the fact that Ernest Holmes' teaching was more than just *essentially* the same from the earliest days to the end of his life, as when Dr. Armor observes:

> As a matter of fact, as I read over the words that he wrote many years later, I find that he was saying the same thing on his last day on this earth that he was saying when I first met him.

This is important, as are Dr. Armor's references to the Religious Science textbook, *The Science of Mind*, by Dr. Holmes, as the invariable standard and norm of the teaching—acknowledging its exclusive place.

However, the principal interest of Dr. Armor's book is its distinctive account of what in an earlier publication he refers to as "Ernest Holmes the man." Here we find the extraordinary juxtaposition of uncommon qualities that made Dr. Holmes one of the very few "giants" of the new, nondual, practical metaphysics first sighted and explored by another son of Maine, Phineas Parkhurst Quimby, the nineteenth-century genius and savant who ushered in the first metaphysically *scientific* philosophy-cum-therapeutics.

Dr. Armor's account draws upon his many years of close association with Ernest Holmes, but it was written long after most of the events recounted here first happened. Thus the sections in which he lets Ernest "tell it" are reconstructions based on many hours of private conversation. These, then, are Dr. Armor's recollections, conveyed in a warm, informal manner.

The reader new to Ernest Holmes will at once catch the essence of the man—and no little of the teaching. Those more acquainted with him and with Religious Science will deepen their insights. Of particular interest are such topics as Dr. Holmes' fidelity to, and enforcement of, the integrity of the Science of Mind teaching; his reaction to the 1954 "split" in the Religious Science movement; and the depth of his regard for his protégé Dr. William Hornaday, whose true status is given here as nowhere else. And the reader will be interested in Dr. Armor's assessment of developments in the Religious Science movement after Ernest Holmes' passage from the scene—to which he adds the note "No one will ever take the place of Ernest Holmes, and it would be futile for anyone to try."

Through Reginald Armor's testimony, we come to know, without distortion or obscuration, the author of *The Science of Mind*—that charter of freedom for seekers and finders everywhere—and the story of his teaching movement.

A final word is in order about the genesis of this book. Dr. Armor's procedure was to dictate a series of taped accounts based on his researches and recollections. These were conveyed to his co-author, who assembled a manuscript based on them. The present version is a reworking of this manuscript by myself. The responsibility for revising dates and data, including some long associated with several of the photographs included here, is also mine, based on new research.

ARTHUR VERGARA
Editor

ERNEST HOLMES
1887 – 1960

From early childhood, Ernest Holmes was convinced of the wholeness of God expressing as Spirit or the Presence, and as Universal Law expressing as Power. These were instinctive realizations that prompted him to unceasingly seek verifying answers from every source. What is God, what is life, what are *we*—and what is our place in the scheme of things? These questions constantly stimulated his quest for truth.

He made no personal claim to the discovery of any great truth. But through his balanced approach to life he added his insight of truth to the findings of the great, the good, and the wise of all ages.

His constant search led him to feel very close to an Infinite Presence. He spent many hours and often days of meditation and communion with, as he put it, ''a Power for Good, greater than we are, in the universe, that we can use.'' The observable response of this Power to thought, word, and feeling caused him to explore the field of prayer and mental healing. As a balanced person approaching this subject from the intellectual as well as the emotional and feeling side of mind, he made a great contribution to modern studies and to the demonstration of mental/spiritual mind healing.

In his later years, some of his experiences bordered on the mystical, and I am sure he had flashes of cosmic consciousness. These experiences left him with an unshakable faith and a certainty of conviction arrived at through his intellectual search for truth. He did not talk about these glimpses of Reality and would not admit to being classed as a mystic, although his inspirational writings are evidence that in truth he was.

Dr. Holmes refused to let anyone put him on a pedestal. He said, "All are rooted in the living of life, and you will discover all have feet of clay." His insights led him to believe that we must of necessity live in the objective world of changing conditions and affairs, but that we also have our roots in the great Reality or Wholeness of God-mind or Life, which does not change.

Through his search and times of meditation he had the immovable conviction that he never walked alone; that there is "a light that lighteth every man that cometh into this world." He sought always to walk in this light and depend on it for guidance. Dr. Holmes sensed God everywhere and felt that the guidance of Spirit was a very real experience.

Dr. Holmes knew that in our search for truth and wisdom, we would never understand it all. "Man will never encompass the Infinite; to do so would make him God, which is an impossibility. Besides, who could or would want that responsibility?" he said. He recognized that true wisdom and enlightenment are a continuous spiritual unfoldment from plateau to plateau. He felt that religious conviction and a sensible practice of that conviction should lead us to a happier, more prosperous, and healthier experience of living.

Dr. Holmes was a "practical idealist and an idealistic realist." These were the qualities that made him the great man that he was, who through his teaching and writing changed the lives and influenced—and continues to influence—the thinking of countless thousands of people throughout the world.

R.C.A.

THAT WAS ERNEST

WHO
WAS
ERNEST
HOLMES?

Sometimes you face an identity crisis
    where you want to do your thing but aren't sure
      of the details . . .

Not Ernest Holmes. Ernest started talking
    about what he called The Thing Itself
      and never quit.

Wherever in the Universe you may live,
    by whatever name you call yourself,
      you are recognized by this Thing.

You are never separated from It.
    It knows you; It loves you . . .
      It *is* you.

That's what Ernest Holmes never stopped talking about.

Who *was* Ernest Holmes?
A cocky little vaudevillian who hobnobbed with the rich and
the famous, the desperate and the doomed?
Yes.

A self-taught student who would short-circuit the most
knowledgeable computer with an incessant "Why?"
Yes.

A saint who read everyone's bible and whose contribution to
world peace founded the creedless religion
Emerson predicted America would produce?
That too.

One of a kind . . . *just like you.*

That was Ernest.

This book, about this man, is a "voyage of discovery." And in
discovering Ernest Holmes, you'll discover yourself—again and
again—because the author of *This Thing Called You* made his
own life around the Thing you really are, the only Thing you'll
ever be, the realization of Which will crown your days and
guarantee your years.

So come along. Walk with someone who was only a kid
when he met Ernest, who grew up beside him, worked for him
all his days . . . and said, "Goodbye—'til we meet again."

In these pages, *you* meet him—*now.*

Chapter 1

♦

"LOOK: NO WART!"

It sure looked like a miracle to me—but then, as a twelve-year-old, I had already learned not to believe everything I heard from older fellows; and seeing was not necessarily believing. Yet it not only looked like a miracle—it sounded like one as well.

Junior Hubbard, the Fire Chief's son, had told me that Skinny's warts had been healed. We were at the Venice City playground, where Junior had just introduced me to the boys on the bench beside the baseball diamond. When Junior took his baseman's mit and headed out to the field, I stayed behind to bat after Skinny.

Skinny got on base. Now it was my turn. The ball came faster than I could see it; but I felt it part my hair. "Happy," the umpire, was out in front immediately, while I floundered in the dirt.

"Play by the rules," he admonished the pitcher, who called back, "Aw, it slipped! Sorry." Happy held out his hand to pick me up out of the dirt. "What's your name, son?" he asked.

"Reginald Armor," I answered. He sure didn't *look* like a miracle-worker; but his handclasp was friendly and his smile warm and understanding.

"Well, Reg," he said, "you look OK. Play ball." He went back behind the catcher and I faced the pitcher once more. And once more the ball came at my head—only this time, the end of my bat managed to get in the way of the ball, which dribbled off in front of me. I ran for first base.

There was Skinny, facing me. Startled, he headed for second. I made it to first, while the throw to second was wild, whereupon Skinny rounded second, heading for third.

Anxious to prove myself first time up, I scampered for second and managed to get there—only to see Skinny charging back, unable to beat the throw to third.

"Go back!!" he screamed at me. I dutifully started; but to avoid being tagged by the second baseman, I slid between his legs to touch the base, and couldn't quite reach it. The second baseman tagged me but fell over me at the same time—and in doing so, touched Skinny with the ball in a double play that looked more like a clown act.

Skinny had dived for second; we had faced each other, both of us reaching for the base—and both out. *But I had been close enough to see his hand.* Sure enough, his sunburned hand had white spots on it—just where the warts had been. No warts! It was sure enough a miracle.

Walking home with Junior and me after the game, Happy wouldn't let me call him "mister." He preferred to be called by his first name.

2

"My name is Ernest," he said. "Ernest Shurtleff Holmes. Ernest Shurtleff was a minister who wrote 'Lead On, O King Eternal.' "

"Oh, are you a minister?" I asked.

"No," he laughed. His smile was warm and full of the kind of respect a kid appreciates getting from an adult. No wonder the kids called him "Happy."

"My older brother's a minister, though," he added. "I live with him* and my mother over at the parsonage on the first street north of Windward Avenue. Say, why don't you come over to the church Friday night? We just formed a Boy Scout troop. Junior's Dad is a Fire Chief, and he set up a drill team. We could possibly use another bugler. With the Drum and Bugle Corps, you march and get to wear a uniform."

I don't think I heard a word after "Fire Chief." Imagine having a Dad who was a real live Fire Chief! My own Dad had died three years before. And now I was walking beside a miracle-worker.

"Junior told me about Skinny's warts," I said; "can you really say some magic words and make them go away?"

He stopped and took my hand in his. "There's no magic about it. Do you want this wart to be healed?"

Tears welled up in my eyes. My new stepfather called it "unsightly." I nodded. "I wish I could get rid of it," I mumbled.

"Wishing won't do it." He laid a finger on the wart. "You don't see it now, do you?"

"No," I said, but . . ."

---

*Fenwicke Holmes.

3

"No *buts*," he commanded. "Think of it each day like you see it right now. It's gone isn't it?"

"Yes, but . . ."

"You *do* believe I can remove the wart, don't you?"

I thought of Skinny's hand: no warts. "Did Skinny *really* have warts?"

"Yes."

"He sure didn't have any at second base!"

"I know," Happy nodded wisely. I wanted to believe. I nodded again.

"It's simple," he said. "You don't see the wart right now." I looked. "You practice not seeing it. Think of it each day as being gone."

A few days later, my entire family attended the Pageant of Venice—an extravaganza which was the forerunner of the California Tournament of Roses and to produce which Venice real-estate promoter Abbot Kinney spent lavishly.* No expense was spared, nothing was overlooked.

I eagerly secured a front-row seat just as the fanfare stopped and the curtains parted. There was Ernest Holmes again, Master of Ceremonies, beaming cherubic all over and intoning: "Welcome to Venice, the City of Mirth by the Western Sea!"

I waved my right hand . . . Look: no wart!

My new friend was not only omniscient, all-knowing; he was omnipresent: everywhere!

---

*Kinney—at one time virtual owner of Venice—donated the lot for Fenwicke's church. It was his word that led to Ernest's first job as playground director and opened the way to the Purchasing Office job for him.

The Boy Scout troop at brother Fenwicke's friendly Congregational church was pure heaven to me. I learned to play the bugle and we marched in patriotic parades, loving the martial music, the uniforms, the flags, and the busyness of it all. We went camping and fishing on weekends. Ernest, although not athletically inclined, loved fishing with his brother Guy.

The church parsonage was just a few blocks closer to town than my house, which Ernest passed to and from the City Playground. We were together so much that many thought I was his adopted son. He probably filled the "father-figure" need in my life. Certainly, from the first time I visited the church, we were inseparable.

I had just come from spending three years with an uncle in Virginia, after the death of my father. There I learned a healthy respect for the Devil and the fires of Hell. The safest thing for a twelve-year-old, then, seemed to be to join the nearest church. The "Holmes" church was closest—and it was different. So were the people who went there. I recall Mrs. Augusta Rundel—affectionately called Gussie—and her sister, "Aunt Annie" —and Aunt Annie's pretty daughter, Hazel. They would all become important parts of my story—because of Ernest Holmes.

Gussie always had to have a cause, and in those Venice years Ernest became one of her projects. Since Ernest headed the Scout troop, Gussie saw to it that we all trooped to town to be fitted for those handsome uniforms. She also helped Ernest pick out his first Scoutmaster's uniform.

Our Scout activities were spurred on by America's involvement in the fast-moving conflict in Europe that became World War I. The troop accompanied bond rallies and savings drives that helped finance the war effort. Everywhere we went, Ernest spoke to crowds. There was a very real flow of energy from him to them, and from them back to him. Later this would be called *charisma*. He had it. In part, it was an affinity with life and living. But more than that, it was Ernest's typical joy, enthusiasm, spontaneity—and an endless seeking and searching.

One day, after the drumming had ceased and the bugles had been put away, Ernest put his arm around my shoulder. "How's school coming, Reg?" he asked.

I was having a hard time adjusting to the situation both at home and at school, but I wasn't going to admit it; so I replied vaguely, "Oh, all right, I guess."

To one sensitive to the needs of others, my tone of voice must have said more than the words did. As a consequence, the walk home that evening took longer as we talked of many things—deep, heady things. And the more we spoke, the further away seemed my problems.

Somehow our conversation touched on life and death, right and wrong, good and evil, justice and injustice, humanity's goodness and humanity's *in*humanity.

Ernest had some very unusual ideas, or so I thought at the time. Instead of problems, we concentrated on solutions—and my own problems were solved: gone just like the wart.

We had walked past my house, had cookies and milk at his house, and watched the rays of the setting sun pour through the stained glass windows of the church where his brother Fenwicke taught.

"We must keep on keeping on," he said of schooling. "Life

itself is a school of perpetual learning—a continuous seeking, seeking, seeking. There is nothing new under the sun. What has been known by only the few in generations past must now be known by the many. Cobwebs are now being brushed away from the corridors of time. Man must learn to understand the great laws that govern his life; he is no longer to be governed by anything outside of himself. Governments, organizations, institutions, creeds, doctrines, churches are all changing to give place to the realization of the individual. All that does not measure up to this standard must fall by its own weight.''

The last ray of light through the stained glass window was most strangely playing out across his brow, and his entire face struck me as illumined, his eyes blazing with their own soft light as he spoke.

''The time is at hand,'' he concluded. ''We are in the greatest age of all history: the time of unifying all people and all things. The whole world must know the truth; and the truth *will* set them free.''

All his life, Ernest Holmes would speak in much that same vein. These particular words were well suited to a boy my age; but variants on them, richer and fuller, would go out to reach many thousands and would serve to lead just where he pointed them. And that very day I resolved to follow where my Scoutmaster led.

Soon, Ernest was accepting out-of-town speaking engagements —something for which he had had training back in his native New England and at which he had earned a little money. He never allowed these trips to conflict with his service at the church; but his curiosity took him to different places as well as to different ways of thinking; and there was nothing that could resist his insistent questioning. As always, I was thrilled to have him tell me about the things he read and the places where he spoke.

Ernest now had a job at the Venice City Hall, where he worked in the office of the Purchasing Agent. This job allowed him plenty of time for reading and study, devouring politics, science, philosophy, religion, and metaphysics. I never called on him there, but an image nonetheless persists of the questioning student behind the closed door marked "Purchasing Agent" with feet propped up on the desk and surrounded by books.

One of the writers that most interested Ernest was the English metaphysician Thomas Troward. Ernest introduced me to Troward's *Edinburgh Lectures on Mental Science*, a work that was beginning to have an impact on thinking people of the time. Grappling to comprehend knowledge beyond my years, I nevertheless was fascinated by what I *could* grasp. By my fourteenth birthday I was hooked, having read all of Troward's books. Of course there were many rereadings ahead of me.

Needless to say, Ernest and many of us were misunderstood for our "radical" ideas—*radical* meaning different from others' opinions. After all, a kid of fourteen talking about the power of Mind to heal the sick and change one's life? And what was this *mind* with a capital *M*? The neighborhood druggist was overheard saying to my mother, "You'd better watch that son of yours. He's a nice boy, BUT . . ." His voice trailed off and his eyes rolled as his forefinger circled his ear, implying, "He's not quite there!" Mother had heard this from others, but fortunately she wasn't impressed or ever offended.

Hearing of the incident, Ernest commented: "Each soul must discover for himself that he stands in the midst of an eternal creative Power which presses Itself around his own thought and casts back at him all that he thinks." To some orthodox elders, that sounded vaguely like a new religion. It would become one—although at that time in his life, Ernest would have been appalled by the suggestion that he was fashioning one. Yet I knew within myself that one day Ernest would do just that.

All of Ernest's life was a time for reading, studying, questioning, probing, digging, often far into the night; and this would not go unnoticed. Across the hallway from the Purchasing Agent's office was another office. Its sign read, "H. B. Aiken, City Engineer." H. B. resembled a beardless Abraham Lincoln, and his merry eyes belied his meager physique.

One day, he crossed the hall to borrow some pipe tobacco from Ernest, who was, as usual, knee-deep in books. "Holmes," he asked, "do you actually read all these?"

"Sure," answered Ernest, refilling his pipe from the green Edgeworth tin. "Take home any I'm not reading in just now." That might not have left much; but take one he did, and two days later he was back in Ernest's office.

"Say, Holmes . . . I'm having a few friends over to the house tonight. Why don't you come over and tell us something about this," he said, pointing to some metaphysical titles.

And that's the way it all began. "That was the first talk on metaphysics I ever gave," Ernest would long remember. It led to others in the homes of other friends.

One evening a woman told him, "You're better than any of the people we hear downtown at the big Metaphysical Library at Broadway and Third. We've spoken to the librarian about you and we've decided you should speak there next Thursday. Admission could be one quarter.''

A classroom-size hall on the ninth floor of the Brack Shops, at Grand Avenue and Seventh Steet, rented for $1.00. Ernest calculated it would take only four attendees to break even, and he was assured of those. So why not talk on his study of the *Edinburgh Lectures*? As it happened, two dozen people showed up on the fateful Thursday that launched a career; and Ernest demonstrated a little prosperity too: after paying for the hall, he went home with five dollars.

Here, as later and elsewhere, an audience would remember his words long after they'd forgotten that his hair was disheveled, his suit crumpled. ''Judge not according to the appearance,'' says the Gospel. *Being* was more important to Ernest Holmes than the *appearance* of being.

The opportunity came for Ernest to speak in San Francisco. The trouble was, our troop had for months been planning a scouting weekend for exactly the same date. Never one to refuse opportunity's knock at the door, Ernest insisted on keeping both commitments. It was evidently important for him to accept the engagement in San Francisco—but he told none of us about it. Instead, we were going camping at what seemed to us the opposite end of the world. But we were eager for the great adventure.

Thus when it came time to break camp and return to ''civilization,'' we were very reluctant to leave. But our Scoutmaster was apparently in some hurry, poking his head in our tents to see that mess kits were packed and bedrolls stowed away, all the while glancing at his watch. And still no word of the speaking engagement.

Like the good Scouts we were, we quickly loaded our gear into the Model T Ford and were off. We had camped near Tioga Pass, and once over the pass, our route would be mostly downhill to the big city and our destination. But the weather was unseasonably hot, and the sun had evaporated much of the water in the car's radiator.

The Model T crawled up the pass and then, with a thud, stopped. "Sounded like a transmission band," said the driver. Assistant Scoutmaster Guy Holmes—Ernest's wiry older brother —was a whiz at mechanics and knew just what to do. The Model T had only two gears, and Guy shifted into the lower, wherupon the car groaned and moved a few feet farther and then BING!—the other transmission band went out.

Ernest's blood was boiling. He sat on the running-board, mopping his brow and puffing from the rarefied altitude and unaccustomed exertion. "Boy!" he exclaimed. "If Hell is anything like this, I'm glad I don't believe in it. I've had it! You boys can do what you want."

Relieved of adult supervision, we did the only thing possible: turn the car around and make our way backwards up the hill, using the only remaining gear: *reverse*. We then coasted down toward the community on the other side of the pass, and once on level ground proceeded in reverse to the nearest car shop. The owner greeted us wide-eyed as we backed into his shop.

"Not fixable today" was his verdict.

"Can we swap transmissions?" Ernest asked, specifying his

city engagement. The mechanic shook his head *No*. Ernest then turned loose all his powers of persuasion. Soon we were on our way.

Arriving in good time, we filed into the rear of the building where the lecture was to take place—just as the announcer was saying, "Yes . . . I think that's our speaker now, treading down the aisle . . . and . . . here he is: Ernest Holmes!"

Sure enough, there he was, mounting the platform—and still in his Scoutmaster's uniform.

That was Ernest.

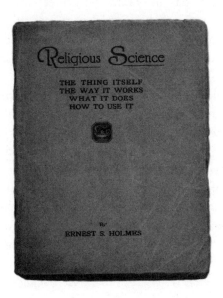

Chapter 2

◆

"WHY? WHY? WHY?"

T HE NAME Abraham Lincoln stands as a worldwide symbol of emancipation and freedom. Perhaps it was significant that Lincoln, Maine, was the birthplace of Ernest Holmes. The small farm where he was born that cold morning of January 21, 1887, wasn't too far removed from the drabness of Lincoln's early years.

Ernest himself tells us:

Being the youngest of nine sons of William and Anna Heath Holmes was a definite advantage in those days. There were no girls' clothes to pass down, and I had the pick of hand-me-downs from seven brothers—Wallace, Luther, William, Charles, Fenwicke, Guy, and Jerome. (Harry passed on in infancy.)

Mother taught school in Lincoln and was a great believer in formal schooling. I recall that I did complete all six grades of grammar school that were offered in Lincoln, just as my brothers did before me, plus some schooling at Gould's Academy in Bethel, Maine. But I did quit school when I was about fifteen and didn't go back except to study public speaking.

This was a large family, a close-knit, congenial group of souls under one roof. Short of stature they were, but dedicated to learning under Mother Holmes' strict New England brand of guidance. Brother Fenwicke later earned a Ph.D.—whereas brother Ernest quit school at fifteen. Yet to say that he quit learning would be the misstatement of all time.

Brother Guy would later say that Ernest's first word was not "Mama" or "Daddy" but "*Why*?" He was a voracious reader; and not only did he absorb the clothing handed down from seven brothers, but he absorbed the information that they possessed.

At an early age he exhibited a life-long characteristic. He would ask a question and, seemingly never satisfied with the answer, would restate the question. He would even seem to argue with himself, seeking the *why* of things, the *how* of things— continually asking Why? Why? Why? sometimes to the point of making a nuisance of himself.

By the turn of the century, economic promptings had moved all the Holmes boys out into the world. Even Ernest, a precocious thirteen years of age, found a summer job at the nearby paper-pulp mill which had given his father intermittent employment over the years.

The loggers and mill-hands were a motley crew, hardworking, hard-drinking, hard-headed, and profane. Some seemed to resent Ernest's urge to ask questions and could be very articulate in their own way when they found Ernest from time to time tucked in some corner, reading away.

Again, Ernest:

In those days New England, theologically, wasn't too far from witch-burning times. Mother was pretty strict, but she tempered this with wisdom, and she determined that we should never be taught that there was anything to be afraid of. Mother just refused to have her family recognize fear.

From the beginning, I was a nonconformist, asking so many questions that my relatives would tear their hair in frustration. But I never stopped asking, then or later. Except for the eternal questioning, I wasn't strange in any way. I had no visions, no hallucinations, met no God who said, "Psst! I'm going to tell you what I haven't told anyone else!" I early concluded that there can be no secrets in Nature, no special Providence, no special dispensations.

I did discover Ralph Waldo Emerson on my own initiative, and I drank him in like a thirsty traveler. His writings were lifelong friends from my eighth birthday on, read and reread many times.

At the mill I had been nicknamed "Happy." I was always humming a tune. You might catch a few words of it and tell which tune; but really nobody knew what the tune was, because actually I couldn't even carry a tune. It was hum, hum, hum, whistle, whistle, whistle.

This combination irritated Big Pierre one Monday morning as he lumbered into the mess hall, red-eyed and short-tempered. Big Pierre was a French-Canadian, a veritable mountain of a backwoodsman, a real-life Paul Bunyan, whose six-foot-nine stature towered over everyone, even sitting down.

But this day he was in no mood to confront anyone who was happy. He picked me up by the seat of the britches and held me at arm's length facing his little deep-set, beady eyes in their forest of black beard, spilling the porridge that I was carrying all over the latest clothing bequest from my next oldest brother.

"Hoppy," he bellowed, "cut out that domn wheestling or I stomp you like an ant!" and he dropped me face down in the widening pool of oatmeal, to the great delight of everyone present.

Anger welled within the small package like a hurricane.

"You big moose!" I shouted; "it's a good thing my father isn't here!"

"Hah!" scoffed Goliath; "dot leetle peanut!"

That did it! He might ridicule me but not my father! I kicked him on the shin and headed down the long hallway.

Letting out a roar like a gored bull, he headed in hot pursuit. I was no match for the giant steps. The giant bent down to pluck my pudgy legs from under me, and we ran out of moving room at the end of the building simultaneously.

I reversed field and scurried back between his legs as his lowered head collided with the stone wall like a battering ram. He stood to his full height and turned around, and his eyes had a glazed expression. I turned and faced him.

"Curse you! You will fall flat on your face!" I cried; and he *did*—straight out, all six-foot-nine of him, with three foot of arm outstretched at my feet.

Someone at the table had called, "Timber-r-r-r!" just in time; and they all had a healthy respect for my word from that day on.

I began to have some inkling that the word of man is creative—always creative—but do we create destruction in anger? It was one of the few times I really let anger explode.

I actually was impatient with formal education. I read anything and everything that I could get my hands on, but I never graduated from the two-year course at Gould's Academy. During the Christmas holidays I overheard my mother and father talking one night about the struggle that brother Fenwicke was having in acquiring his college education. It was their life's dream for him to become a minister. Perhaps every family in lower economic circumstances aspires to have a doctor, a lawyer, a minister, or some really completely educated person in the family.

"Well," I thought, "if my brother needs to be subsidized, certainly *I* don't need anybody to take care of *me*." Instead of returning to the Academy after the

Christmas holidays, I resolved to go down and visit my cousins in Boston who had a butcher shop.

To avoid some frustrating debate with my parents in the matter, I neglected to discuss it with them but instead left them a note saying that I had been called to the big city as an apprentice in the butcher shop.

The spirit of independence was high in me at that time, as no doubt it is high in every fifteen-year-old— the feeling, the desire, the urge to be free of parental counsel and advice, to make one's own way in the world and not be dependent on anything or anybody.

Boston was the cradle of American independence. It was where the Tea Party had started the whole thing, and I was resolved to have my own personal Tea Party. I was welcomed by my cousins in Boston, where we had visited several times before. They seemed glad to see me and welcomed having the extra hand of an apprentice "bootcher" as they called it in their New England accent. I was full of questions and learned quickly.

There was an outstanding minister at a neighboring church in Boston that I wanted to meet, so I went over there for service one Sunday and stayed after the service to meet the man. My reading had already outstripped his theology and I made a pest of myself asking him questions about God, immortality, and so forth. Most of his answers were really not very satisfactory. I knew that this was one questioner he was glad to usher to the door.

The eager, questioning mind sometimes created problems for me. The ceaseless, eternal questioning was

18

not always looked upon with favor by those whom I questioned, especially when they didn't have the answers —or when their answers were based on superstition, dogma, or "Well, it's so because the Book says it's so," or "Because so-and-so says it's so!" I just wasn't interested in third-party experiences. I felt as though I had to experience this thing myself, *each* thing myself.

Later on at the Venice City Hall, my good friend H. B. Aiken, the City Engineer, was working on the plans for a new sewer line one day at the same time as I was reading a very challenging book. We had debated Chapter 2 the night before, and the debate continued across the hall between our two offices throughout the day.

I would pop into H. B.'s office every few minutes with another question and he would take time from his drawing board to answer me. Finally, in exasperation, he threw his pen down and exclaimed, "Questions, questions, questions! Now *I'm* going to ask *you* a question, Holmes, and I don't want you to come back in here until you have figured out the answer, you understand? Now for Pete's sake, will you tell me: Why don't elephants roost in trees?" He ushered me to the door, and there were no more questions that day.

You see? That was Ernest.

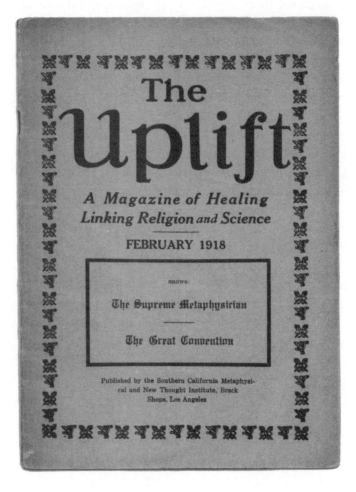

The Uplift

A Magazine of Healing
Linking Religion and Science

FEBRUARY 1918

SHOWS:

The Supreme Metaphysician

The Great Convention

Published by the Southern California Metaphysical and New Thought Institute, Brack Shops, Los Angeles

Chapter 3

◆

"I JUST CHECKED WITH THE CHEF"

NEXT DOOR to the butcher shop was a grocery store, and next door to that, on the corner, an apothecary shop. Across the street was a bakery. Next door, the other way, was a cobbler and a candlemaker. In the food business Ernest ate well and had a roof over his head, surrounded by interesting people—"the butcher, the baker, the candlestick-maker." None was free from the inquiring mind of youth. No trade secret was so sacred as to be exempt from probing discussion any weekday, and nothing sacred was sacrosanct on Sunday, when the week's work was done.

Boston was a melting pot. The Catholic Irish were well represented. But every Protestant faith was there as well, including the descendants of the original Pilgrims and Puritans. Quakers, Unitarians, agnostics, and atheists mingled alike with Baptists, Presbyterians, Methodists, and Evangelicals. There were old historic synagogues. There were East Indians from the ships in the harbor. The Buddhist way was not unknown, and the many sons and daughters of the local Chinese restaurateur were among the Sunday crowds strolling in the park.

The young people liked to gather after church at the apothecary shop on the corner. The boys and girls would meet and mingle over an ice-cream delight or perhaps a soda shared courtingly with two straws.

I'll let Ernest himself tell this next part, for it is the only time I ever heard him mention a girl in his early life.

One Sunday I contrived an introduction by a mutual acquaintance to "that girl." Since it was Sunday, in the course of our conversation I discreetly inquired as to her religion. "My folks practice their religion *every* day," she replied haughtily. "We're Christian Scientists, you know. There's a whole group of Christian Scientists at my school."

The very term *scientist* stirred my imagination. Science implied the asking of questions. Isn't this what I have always done? I asked myself. "Have another soda," I suggested, "and tell me all about it." At 6:59 that evening, the old gentleman who operated the business wanted to close the shop to attend prayer meeting and there were 12 empty soda glasses and I had only fifty cents in my pocket. Sensing my embarrassment, "that girl" generously offered to lend me ten cents so we could "leave graciously," as she put it. Reluctantly, I accepted, but only on condition that I be permitted to escort her to her church next week. Her gracious acceptance sent a warm glow through me. Wasn't Science wonderful!

Perhaps the passion for perfection and the free use of abundance were only reactions to my early years of lack and the spreading of the meager family substance over many mouths and many backs. I loved to spend liberally and bought quality and value over display and show. Wasn't the grocer next door rich, having a whole stock of bananas to sell over the long New England winters? Didn't the Holy Bible say, "Freely you have received, freely you should give"?

In Maine we were lucky to have a banana in *summertime*, and here I could get one any time I had a spare coin. Of course, how free was free? By the way, was the Holy Bible really the holy word of God, or had it suffered many translations by mere man?

More questions!

Another lifelong habit of Ernest's was going to the source for information. This I can illustrate with an amusing incident that took place years later at a restaurant frequented by my wife and myself, to which we brought Ernest as our guest. He was looking over the menu while I ordered a steak.

"Do they serve a good steak?" he questioned.

"I've always found it to be pretty good, but I don't know how you'll like it," I offered.

"Wait just a minute," said Ernest, and he popped up and disappeared. In a few moments he came back to the table and said, "Yes, that steak is all right." He knew meat, and he was satisfied.

In my mind's eye I could see him going into the kitchen, sticking his finger into the steak, and testing its quality and tenderness. Any other person doing that would probably be chased out in no uncertain terms by the chef flourishing a meat cleaver. But Ernest was well liked by man and boy. Of course, he never did forget the lessons he learned as a "bootcher" (he still used the New England pronunciation).

This was the man, Ernest—a unique individual demonstrating the common touch that he had with all people. He had the faculty of making everyone think that they were his very best friends. And in a sense they truly were, because that is how he felt about other people.

"Yes," he said jovially, "that steak is all right. I just went out to the kitchen and checked with the chef."

That was Ernest.

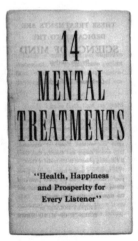

Chapter 4

◆

CHAUTAUQUA DAYS

O NE NIGHT, after hearing the Reverend Russell H. Conwell deliver his famous "Acres of Diamonds" speech at Boston's famous Lyceum, Ernest waited until the last person had left the hall. The Reverend Conwell had said that "you have no right to be poor"—a challenging thought indeed to the lad whose generous nature hardly permitted keeping a coin from payday to payday.

Many people had clustered around the speaker with requests for his autograph. Few had the audacious questions of this youth who would not be denied. The Reverend Conwell rose to the challenge.

"*Of course* I belive that the 'Acres of Diamonds' are right where you are! Opportunity is everywhere present. Set a high price on yourself, my boy. I ask for $200 a night. I get it. I give it away."

Ernest was impressed. $200 a night was a lot, and to the lad from the "bootcher" shop, it was a fortune *just for speaking—* his favorite pastime!

His healthy respect for education took note that it was the *Reverend* Mr. Conwell. Well, his brother Fenwicke, four years his senior, would soon be a Reverend. Perhaps it was time he acquired more formal education himself. These were the days when James Redpath's Lyceum Bureau booked organized programs of winter entertainment in all the larger cities and Keith Vaughter's "summer culture" did week-long programs under the big tent in thousands of Main Streets U.S.A.

They called this tent culture "Chautauqua," after the summer cultural resort in southwest New York, and the lecture was the main event. The lecturers included politicians and preachers, actors, authors, sculptors. There were also the Dunbar Bell Ringers, Hungarian bands, girls' choruses, "lightning cartoonists," magicians, puppeteers, quick-change impersonators, hoofers, and stand-up comedians.

But the edifying lecture was the program's backbone, and it was the day of the inspirational lecturer. One good lecture, forever repeated, might suffice a speaker forever. If it had the right touch, the right emotional lift; if it started a tear down the face of the nice old lady down in the third row; if a few brash young men stumbled out of the tent vowing to take a hand the next day in making this a better world; its creator could stay on the Chautauqua circuit for years. Some of them did for life.

Attracted by show business, Ernest, with characteristic thoroughness, resolved to show up at the Leland Powers School of the Spoken Word the following Monday morning. Never satisfied with less than the best, if the lecturer was the number one spot, then he would be a lecturer.

Mr. Powers was known as a "reader"—a recitalist, we might say today: he was the originator of a special form of play-reciting on the platform. He could condense a play, say by Shakespeare, to less than an hour's time, speaking and even acting all the parts—and filling the Boston Lyceum. "Reader," perhaps; but he was every bit the actor, from the top of his erudite head to the tips of his shining patent leather pumps. *And* he was founder and principal of the Leland Powers School of the Spoken Word—as well as the author of *Talks on Expression* and *Fundamentals of Expression*. How could Ernest, himself a great-speaker-to-be, not be impressed?

As for Mrs. Powers, she too was a "reader"—but of a different sort. A woman of breeding and great personal charm, she was the Second Reader of The Mother Church of the Christian Science organization in Boston. The Second Reader read from the Bible during Christian Science services on Sunday; and The Mother Church was the "premier" church for Christian Scientists around the world.

Mr. and Mrs. Powers took an immediate liking to Ernest and in a sense adopted this grown-up little farmboy, taking him under their wing. At the Powers' home, Ernest was surprised to find, beside the typically prominent Bible in the family parlor, another black-leatherbound book, equally prominent, titled *Science and Health*, by Mary Baker Eddy—the founder of Christian Science. Always interested in unlocking life's mysteries, he browsed in it.

He would go home with a borrowed copy of this Christian Science textbook and pore over it with diligence and fascination. But his reaction to the healing philosophy was that anything that anyone had ever done, anyone else could do. There could be no secrets in Nature.

> This I have always believed: There's no special providence, no God who says, "Now, Ernest, you have been a good boy, so I am going to tell you what I didn't tell any others." Of course not. Whatever man has done, man can do. *I* am man, and *I* can do these things.

Ernest's acquaintance with Mr. & Mrs. Powers opened new horizons to his expanding young consciousness. And Boston itself, as a center of culture, was beckoning. To Ernest, it was a long, long way from the country schoolhouse in Maine. Here were answers to some of his questions—answers that stimulated even more questions.

Meanwhile, Ernest was "Chautauqua-bound." During his early experience, he found it difficult to sleep the night before an engagement, and he was all tied up in knots until the very time he spoke. Then once he started talking, it was free and easy and very relaxed.

Ernest used to say that there is a lot of ham in everybody, and one very dramatic reading that goes back to Chautauqua days was his recitation of "Mother o' Mine," which in later years he recited annually on Mother's Day. The tears would roll down his cheeks as he would point upward and intone:

> If I were hanged on the highest hill,
>   Mother o' mine, O Mother o' mine,

I know whose love would be with me still,
Mother o' mine, Mother o' mine.

Then he would wipe away the tears and jolt everyone back to the reality of the moment by saying with a laugh, "Isn't it terrible to see a fat man cry?" and this would bring down the house with laughter.

After a brief experience with Chautauqua and dramatics, Ernest decided that this was not for him. Whenever Ernest's consciousness outgrew the thing he was doing, he simply walked away from it. And when he left something behind him, he was always through with it. He never looked back when he felt the urge, the call, to bigger things.

That was Ernest!

ANNOUNCING

A COURSE OF LESSONS IN
THE LAWS OF

THE ABSOLUTE

HEALING - PROSPERING
BLESSING - LOVING

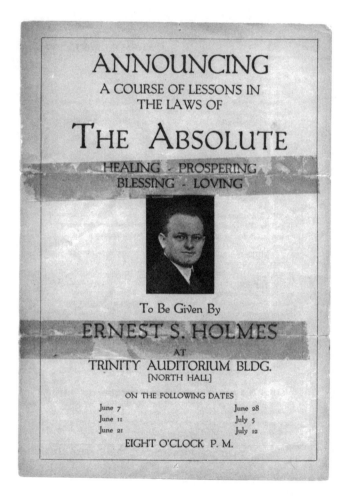

To Be Given By

ERNEST S. HOLMES

AT

TRINITY AUDITORIUM BLDG.
[NORTH HALL]

ON THE FOLLOWING DATES

June 7	June 28
June 11	July 5
June 21	July 12

EIGHT O'CLOCK P. M.

Chapter 5

♦

CALIFORNIA DESTINY and STRIPED TROUSERS

Brother Fenwicke had been ordained a minister, and in 1910, seeking a warmer climate for reasons of health, had settled in the Los Angeles suburb of Venice, where he became a home missionary and built a small, thriving church.

Fenwicke's letters had spoken glowingly of Los Angeles' constant good weather and the rich scenery. In 1912 Ernest, then twenty-five and fresh from his Chautauqua experience, thought that it might be worthwhile to make an exploratory visit to California to do dramatic readings in churches.

"Go West, young man," advised John Soule of the Terre Haute, Indiana, *Express* in 1851—counsel later reinforced by Horace Greeley's oratory. Perhaps a young man should heed the alluring advice and do what it said to do!

He found Los Angeles an exciting place, a growing city of progressive people in a ferment of expanding their horizons, not only physically but mentally and spiritually. It was a community of stimulating intellectuals. Anything that anyone might want to study was taught there. And he did study! He read and studied everything he could get a hold of—no one single thing. From the beginning, as he later put it, "I didn't take one bondage away from myself only to create another. I have always been very careful about that."

Especially of interest, though, was what went by the name of New Thought. Its groups and even organizations were going strong in California, particularly in the San Francisco and Los Angeles areas. But New Thought had its strength elsewhere as well—Kansas City; Chicago; New York; Boston; and in many other cities and even some out-of-the-way places—wherever its gospel had spread.

And what was its gospel? New Thought was in some ways a parallel movement to Christian Science. It traced its origin to the same man who had healed Mary Baker Eddy: Phineas Parkhurst Quimby. But whereas Mrs. Eddy had her own "revelation," theology, and exclusive church organization, New Thought made no such claims. It was looser, more open, and based as much as possible on *results* rather than on the additional element of somebody's theology and revelation.

The dictionary calls New Thought

a mental healing movement, embracing a number of small groups and organizations devoted generally to such

32

ideas as spiritual healing, the creative power of constructive thinking, and personal guidance from an inner presence.

Although in many ways inadequate (e.g. "a presence" instead of "*the* Presence"), the definition is based in part on an early statement of purpose of the International New Thought Alliance:

> to teach the Infinitude of the Supreme One; the Divinity of man and his infinite possibilities through the creative power of constructive thinking and obedience to the voice of the indwelling Presence, which is our source of Inspiration, Power, Health and Prosperity.

Brother Fenwicke, Ernest found, was also interested in the New Thought movement. He had read books by William Walker Atkinson, one of the early New Thought writers, whose pen name was Yogi Ramacharaka. Not satisfied with a metaphysical correspondence course he and Fenwicke had taken jointly with the later New Thought figure Christian D. Larson, Ernest went directly to a Christian Science practitioner in Los Angeles and said, "I want to know what you know."

His early reading had convinced him that no one of the Truth Movement leaders or doctrines contained the whole truth. Perhaps the whole truth was too much for one person. He early began toying with the idea of *synthesis*.

Fenwicke was busy with a municipal election, and Ernest helped him. (Their candidate won a judgeship.) The brief encounter with politics convinced Ernest that most people are largely controlled by outer suggestions rather than inner realizations. He thought that no living soul can demonstrate two different things at the same time, like the man who got on the horse and rode off in all directions. He said, "See, hear, talk, read, only about what you wish. God must become your one great Reality—not simply as a principle of life, but more as the great Mind which knows and which at all times understands and responds."

Of healing, Ernest said:

> What of the daily contact with life—the busy street, the marketplace? We are still creating the word and sending it afloat in the great ethers of life. Are these words creating for us? Yes. It is not from the teaching but from the being that true greatness comes. To heal, we must mentally see perfection. Realize that your word destroys everything unlike itself. . . .
>
> Live the Truth. Be the Truth. You have no responsibility to save the world, except by exemplifying the truth. The world must save itself. The past is gone when we learn to forgive and to forget. The new order, peace, takes the place of confusion. Faith answers the cry of doubt and fear. The Word is supreme.

Ernest's idea of a "Chautauqua" circuit, using churches as his lecture platform, did not quite materialize, and Fenwicke's creative urges took several directions outside the pulpit. But the brothers were kept close by their interest in the metaphysical approach to healing—both of the body and of human affairs.

Holmes-brothers debates sometimes went far into the night. Mother Holmes lived with them at the roomy, comfortable, two-storey parsonage in the canal section of Horizon and Riviera streets. Small, thin, wizened, she lived to be ninety-nine. Always bustling with energy and quick of tongue, she would express her opinion of all the parties to the debates and then retire for the night.

One thing all the brothers did agree on was the need for "uplift," for by 1916 the turmoil of war in Europe was being felt worldwide. "Turbulence in the material world only reflects the turmoil of the spirit in the inner world," mused Ernest one evening after supper.

"Uplift" had been preached from Fenwicke's pulpit that Sunday. Ever willing to practice their preaching, the two brothers decided uplift needed a wider forum than the small church, so together they launched a publication titled, naturally, *Uplift*. The print media (the only "media" then) were publishing all the negative happenings and disseminating all the downward trends. Let's lift the attention and focus it upward, thought Ernest.

Taking their philosophy even further, and applying their ideas on healing, they started a sanitarium at Long Beach with nurses—and with practitioners using spiritual mind healing as outlined in Ernest's first book, *Creative Mind* (1918). There were many wonderful healings and many other wonderful results.

Feeling the taste of public acceptance, Ernest never again worked for anyone else. He had studied and studied and questioned and asked; he had gotten answers; and now he felt that he knew enough about his subject to open an office in Venice and set up a metaphysical practice. "I'm going into business now myself. I'm going to be a practitioner of this science of mind-healing."

Gussie Rundel ("Aunt" Gussie, we called her; for she was really like an aunt to us—a successful real-estate dealer and socialite), Fenwicke, and other friends got together and had a beautiful office furnished on the second floor of the Sibley Building. As Ernest related it, he went to this beautiful office and sat there and sat there, and nothing happened . . . absolutely nothing. Nobody came around, and one day he finally said, "This is it, I've had it. I'll never do this again. I will never have an office. I will never speak publicly unless someone comes to me and says, 'We are ready for you.' This thing either works or it doesn't— and if it does, it's a hundred percent; it does not fail."

Of course, a professional man couldn't ethically advertise in those days, and people were just not aware that help was available, even though they had the need. This, too, pointed out an important lesson to Ernest: that of *letting things happen*; not forcing or straining or pushing to *make* things happen.

Still, he constantly felt urged to larger things. Every new experience brought a new restlessness. Later on, as success piled on success, when a given job was completed and the demonstration made, he was ready to move on to a larger sphere of activity.

For now, his new sphere would be the lecture hall. Ernest was ready for success, and Gussie Rundel knew it was so before it arrived. She had his suits tailor-made and in the very height of fashion. I was on the platform with him throughout his career, and in the early days Ernest insisted that we dress alike on the platform: in winter, the same dark suits; in summer, the same white ones. Thus when he went back to lecturing after his experience as a practitioner, he wore the ultimate in elegance: the cut-away coat and the striped trousers—every inch the visiting dignitary, the voice of wisdom; and every inch of his 5′ 3″.

And that—every inch of him—was Ernest.

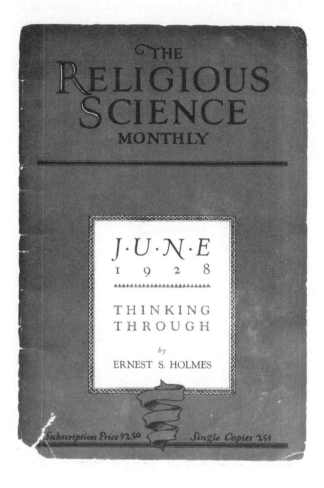

THE
RELIGIOUS
SCIENCE
MONTHLY

J·U·N·E
1 9 2 8

THINKING
THROUGH

by
ERNEST S. HOLMES

Subscription Price $2.50   Single Copies 25¢

Chapter 6

♦

THE
PEOPLE,
THE
CROWDS

THE 1920s were exuberant years in America. After the savagery in Europe, Americans were more than ever interested in higher education and culture. Was not President Woodrow Wilson himself a former college professor? Yes, education and culture enjoyed a status in this country as never before.

These years in Ernest Holmes' life were also busy and exuberant. With his brown wavy hair, his little bit of plumpness—not fat; just pleasingly moonfaced, the grown-up cherubic look of a choir boy—he was always up and doing.

People were expansion-minded, and lecturers were in demand on many "expansive" topics, such as science and mind. The Holmes brothers' fame had begun to spread outside California. Both Fenwicke and Ernest had already heard the call of the lecture trail to other pastures which appeared greener. At about that time, Ernest came to me one day and said, "Reg, we have merged *Uplift* magazine with *Truth* magazine, published by Albert Grier, who heads The Church of the Truth, and Fenwicke is arranging to turn the sanitarium over to others."

Ernest had been like a father to me. Perhaps psychologically he did replace my own father, for my stepfather and I were never close as "father and son." Certainly Ernest's feeling toward me could have been no different if he had been my own father.

"Reg," he said, "you have been with me on the platform since the old Boy Scout days. Fenwicke and I are considering signing contracts for a lecture tour of the East. Would you like to go along with me as my assistant?"

My eyes widened with anticipation. Would a fish like to swim? Would a bird like to fly? My imagination went back to the summer before my graduation from high school when Ernest had asked me to accompany him on a transcontinental trip to his family's home town.

We had defrayed expenses of the trip by making several stops en route for speaking engagements. Although I was not yet seventeen, I had taken in tickets at the door, counted money, seen that the money was banked—and acquired some worldly wisdom in the business world, I thought. I had also helped set up the stage and sketched on the blackboard to illustrate his points as Ernest directed me.

What a summer that had been! We visited some of his cousins in Boston—the Steeves—and their sons Roy and Fen (which was short for Fenwicke) were such good fun. I had the opportunity of meeting all the Holmes brothers. His brother Charles was a high school principal in Connecticut at the time. Not being then out of high school myself, I was very impressed. Imagine having a principal in the family!

I believe Walter—the oldest of the eight brothers—never left Lincoln, Maine—the family hometown. Walter had a hardware store and seemed very prosperous. He was growing and storing potatoes on the side at the time, because a potato famine in Europe had made many people conservation-minded.

Walter and brother Luther had invited me on a camping trip to a lake near Lincoln, and I felt very much like one of the brothers myself—perhaps a younger one. The Holmes brothers certainly had the knack of making one feel comfortable in their presence.

Brother Jerome had become a Congregational minister, like Fenwicke, and later he became a missionary to Japan. I recall that during World War II he was quite valuable as an interpreter for the government, owing to his many years of experience with Japanese language and customs. He later taught at the Institute of Religious Science in Los Angeles for several years.

Brother Guy, shorter even than Ernest, was his favorite— less than five feet tall, a wiry little man just full of fun.

Brother William and his family later followed Ernest to the West Coast, where he too helped with the early lectures, as I recall.

These were days when the mind was not yet solely the province of the professional man with medical credentials. The public was interested in the traveling psychologists and "mentalists," and both lectures and discussions frequently centered on the area of psychic phenomena, spiritualism, mind-reading, and hypnotism.

I was eager to be somehow involved in all this, on the road, traveling America. Ernest's invitation to continue on with him met with a ready response.

"Yes, Ernest," I said; "I'll follow wherever you lead." I would have followed him anywhere for free—and here he was offering me expenses and a little pocket money besides. I could hardly wait for my high school graduation, because I sensed that this experience would be unlike anything that had gone before. And so it was.

The people, the crowds, were the beginning of a new phase, a phase of evolving growth in the life of Ernest Holmes as I knew him—and in the life of Reginald Armor.

The discussion of evolution, and of *evolving* in general, was much on the public tongue in those days. Ernest said that the impulse back of evolution must be a divine urge toward self-expression. This intelligent Life Principle is conscious of itself as evolving. The Principle of Life itself is *arbitrary as law* but *spontaneous as volition*.

In the process of evolution whenever there is a demand for anything, that thing emerges. "We know," Ernest said, "that there are lower forms of intelligence in the order of evolution than man, and there may be beings more highly evolved than we are."

In the year 1920, Ernest spoke on the same platform with Doctor W. John Murray in New York City, Philadelphia, and Boston. Murray was one of the most influential New Thoughters of the period and pastor of New York's prestigious Church of the Healing Christ (later, the "Emmet Fox" church). Everywhere we went, from the platform all I could see was a sea of faces. People were seeking. They were asking questions even as earlier Ernest had asked questions. He was in his element. He loved every minute of it, and so did I.

As a general rule, Fenwicke would alternate with Ernest on the platform. One night one would speak, and the next night the other. Ernest was always interested in the Mental Science teaching, and after the lectures (which were free) had drawn full audiences to the theater, he would hold classes. Sometimes as many as a thousand people would attend a lecture, with many enrolling for the series of lessons at a $25 fee.

The Holmes brothers were demonstrating prosperity; Fenwicke spoke of investments in land, businesses, and stocks. They also explored Eastern philosophies, including the practice of yoga; and although Fenwicke was quite impressed with the dietary aspects of some, Ernest never deviated from his original inspiration and intent. In fact, as I read over words that he wrote many years later, I find that he was saying the same thing in his last days on this earth as he was saying when I first met him.

Reality never changes; the great verities of life are the same yesterday, today, and tomorrow. This is the only Truth that Ernest would admit. By Reality he meant the limitless possibility back of all accomplishments—the cosmic Intelligence back of all manifestation. This reality includes within itself all past, present, and future. Call it Mind, call it God, call it "the Thing Itself." There is only one Reality, and all reality is One.

But if Reality wasn't changing, the times certainly were. In 1924 the traveling platform lecture extolling culture and uplift reached its peak. That year, there were 12,000 separate Chautauquas experienced by an estimated 30 million Americans out of a total population of 90 million; and Lyceum lectures were at an all-time high. The federal government defined these activities as "amusement" and imposed a 10 percent amusement tax. Meanwhile, the good people of the Chautauqua circuit were about to be replaced by mechanical-reproduction means: *talking* motion pictures! Two years later, much of the available money in the United States was borrowed, and the Florida real estate boom collapsed. Falling land prices caused bank failures the following year, indicating an impending economic crisis.

Ernest and Fenwicke had differences of opinion and never functioned again as the "Holmes Brothers." Late in 1924 Fenwicke answered a call to the pulpit of the Church of the Healing Christ in New York, where he remained for several years. Ernest sensed larger goals; he was ready for a greater experience. He wanted to teach. So he hired a hall and started from scratch on his own.

We launched the beginnings of the Science of Mind as a 52-week study course, with a Sunday lecture on a scientific religious basis. There were those who early considered us to be on the "kooky, lunatic fringe"—but I may say that we got *our* share of kooky, lunatic-fringe people!

The early lectures were rather sparsely attended, as I recall them. However, this did not prevent Ernest from being in rare form—or from having challenges from the floor, as on the night he concluded so magnificently, "The great are great to you because you are on your knees. Arise, and stand on your feet!"

Just then a man in the middle of the audience did arise and stand on his feet, commencing what appeared to be a harangue that lasted several minutes. Ernest stood calmly and listened to him. Then he came out from behind the lectern to the front of the platform and, pointing his finger directly at the man, said, "Listen here, you! *I'm* paying the rent here. If *you* are going to do the speaking, YOU rent the hall!"

Everybody had a great laugh as he proceeded with the lecture.

Ernest typically spoke of an infinite source of all good things and an abundance of supply. While others were talking lack or limitation, Ernest rose above all lack and all limitation, and experienced the abundance of which he spoke. He wanted larger groups *on his own*—not something that he shared with his older brother. And we *had* large groups.

On the platform, he opened his consciousness and let it all happen through him. He spoke of healing—of healing people's bodies *and* the body of their affairs. They listened and they loved it. They told their friends. And their friends told *their* friends. The people kept coming, and the crowds got larger.

Ernest spoke of an infinite Love that knows nothing unlike Itself—and *they* loved *him*.

That was Ernest.

The Institute of · · Religious Science and School of Philosophy offers every student in life's class instruction that will better enable him to meet · the · requirements necessary for admission · into · the upper grades of experience · where · · · · health, harmony and success are mastered

2511 Wilshire Boulevard
Los Angeles, Cal.

Chapter 7

◆

NOT SO "LITTLE" WOMEN

Women exercise a subtle influence in the lives of men, an influence that sometimes is more apparent in retrospect than it was at the time of its happening. Whenever one of the early movies was being filmed in or near Venice, my mother would go over and play extra parts in the crowd scenes. She said that it was great fun, it lent variety to her life, she always met new people; and after the filming was over, the whole crowd was invited over to Gussie Rundel's for a party.

Indeed, "Aunt" Gussie must have resolved to maintain a floating party for her friends at any hour of the day or night. She was a businesswoman, owned several properties, and shared a lavish apartment on the canal with her sister, Ann Durkee Gillan—and no two sisters could be more dissimilar than Ann and Augusta. I never knew a Mr. Rundel or a Mr. Gillan, nor do I recall whether the women were widows or divorcees. It just seems that they were always to me "Aunt Annie" and "Aunt Gussie."

Through Gussie's parties passed a constant parade of the rich and the famous, as well as the talented, the gifted, the creative—and those who were just plain out of work. Prominent people of the silent-movie days came and went. There was J. Paul Getty, barely in his early twenties and already in the oil business. And there was Mrs. Hazel Durkee Foster and her wealthy businessman husband. Matchmakers Gussie and Annie would later, after Mr. Foster's death, encourage Ernest and Hazel; but I am getting ahead of my story.

If Gussie's apartment was busy in the evening, certainly the Holmes "mansion" was no less so in the daytime. The sanitarium in Long Beach was sold, and a big, rambling house in Los Angeles on Third Avenue, just off Adams Boulevard, was bought. Into it moved the entire Holmes clan: Mother and Father Holmes; Ernest; Guy and his wife, Emma, together with their son and daughter, Lawrence and Josephine; Fenwicke and his son, Louis—adopted at age six while the family was at the sanitarium; and Agnes Galer, a Divine Science minister from Seattle who would later ordain Ernest so that he could legally conduct weddings and funerals. She was a most unusual person —talented, charming, and very, very intelligent. Later her daughter, Anne, came to join the crowd—one happy family.

Anne, a recent gradute of a teachers' college in the East, in heels stood just a little taller than Ernest and on occasion referred to him as "that crude little vaudevillian" or to the little man's not being polished enough for her. (Her eyes, however, suggested that perhaps she knew someone who was willing to do the polishing.) For his part, Ernest loved everyone. At a party he was great fun—although some of his "party stories" certainly would not do on the platform.

One thing he would no longer do was give a Chautauqua reading. I don't know whether it was that Anne had laughed at his first attempt in her presence, or whether this was indicative of a broken romance in that year before his coming to California.

With a great ear for music and with a comparable appreciation of it, Ernest nevertheless could not carry a tune. His singing, at parties, was in fact so bad that it led to the rumor being circulated that he drank heavily—although I never knew him to take more than a glass or two of wine. In fact, anyone who knew Ernest realized that he was almost a teetotaller. He did not like the stuff, as he used to put it—but he would hasten to add that he had no objection to others taking a drink now and then if they so wished. That was their business—although he had no patience with overindulgence, and minced no words about it.

Ernest's success was Aunt Gussie's special charge almost from the beginning, and either she or Aunt Annie was almost always in the audience whenever he spoke in Los Angeles. So, later, was Ernest's wife, who told of having attended a Sunday lecture at the Wiltern Theatre, where she usually sat in the first balcony, second row.

On this particular day, she overheard two women in the first row conversing. One of them asked, "Who is this Holmes, anyway?"

"Oh, don't you know? He is a *wonderful* speaker! I attended a party, though, after one of his lectures, and I understand he is a very heavy drinker.'' (She had evidently heard Ernest attempt to sing!)

The other woman responded, ''Oh, is that so? The poor thing!''

''Yes,'' the first woman continued, ''it's a pity. And do you know, that to actually get him on the platform they sometimes have to point him in the right direction and give him a push! The strange part of it is, that to hear him speak, you'd never suspect he'd had even one drink! And besides, I hear that his wife writes all of his talks for him!''

What makes this even more ridiculous is the fact that he never wrote a talk or a lecture in his life, much less ever read one that someone had written for him.* This isn't to say that he did not prepare. As a matter of fact, he was *always* prepared.

He would consider his speaking topic early in the week; and although he would say that he never prepared anything, he would ask people their opinions about various ideas on this particular subject churning in his mind all week long. So in fact he not only *was* prepared to speak, but he was *constantly* preparing. And before terribly long, he had years of constant preparation on the subject he loved so well—the Science of Mind.

In his talks, Ernest could soar to the heights emotionally— and then descend immediately to some mundane topic. This was part of his charm in speaking. And it was this charm, plus the sincere, overall balance which was Ernest Holmes, that would

---

*For a relevant and amusing anecdote, see *Collected Essays of George Bendall*, pp. 112, 113.

first arouse people's interest in him and in his lectures in the early days—even though many of those who listened did not fully grasp what he was saying.

Early in his lecture experience he was called on to participate in a funeral service with a Masonic group. I overheard a friend of mine who attended the service tell how much he had liked Ernest's part in it. When I asked my friend just what, in his estimation, the key point was that Ernest brought out in his talk, he replied in all seriousness, "I don't really know. . . . No, I *really don't know* much about what he said; but I sure did like it!"

It was Emerson who said, "What you are speaks so loudly that I cannot hear what you say." Well, what Ernest Holmes was to everyone spoke so loudly that if they didn't completely understand his *words*, they understood *him*; and they loved him. Because one cannot give out love without having love returned. This was especially true of Ernest, who mentally hugged his audience before speaking to them. But to have someone special and personal to hug is important—very important—too. That someone, for Ernest, was Hazel.

A man could not help noticing that Hazel was beautiful of face and form. She had the peaches-and-cream complexion of the true redhead, and her auburn hair shone in the afternoon sun, as did her open, warm, and generous nature. But the most impressive thing about Hazel was her hauntingly beautiful and very piercing eyes of the clairvoyant, the inner vision that sees not only the exterior but looks right through a person. They were framed by heavy eyebrows that focused the attention deep into the windows of the soul.

Hazel was not only lovely to see, gracious and charming to know, but every bit the gentlewoman. Her consciousness was aware of no lack or poverty. They just were not in her experience. She was Ann Durkee's daughter, but she resembled Aunt Gussie more than Aunt Annie. And she mingled easily with the affluent and the influential. She moved with the easy grace of the gazelle, the charm and breeding of the lady of quality and culture.

The first person Ernest met on his first trip to California was Fenwicke; the second person was Hazel. He must have carried her image in his subconscious for many years. Her eyes, as I have already mentioned, were difficult to forget. They proclaimed that life is to be lived. And this I have heard Ernest tell many times:

> I have seen Hazel give away a corsage of orchids to the first person who admired them. Beads—the same way. Hats—if someone admired her hat, she would take it off and say, "It's yours." Rings and jewelry—the same way.

I remember one night, when I was in my first year of high school, I was driving Ernest home after a speaking engagement. He asked me to please drop him off at Aunt Gussie's—there was a party going on, as usual. I later learned that the party went on all night, and I often wondered how Ernest got home afterward.

I also wondered if Mrs. Hazel Foster had been there. Mr. Foster's decease had left her a wealthy widow, and Aunt Gus-

sie suggested a world tour to forget her sorrow (properly chaper-
oned, of course, by her dear Aunt Gussie, who enjoyed travel
almost as much as party-giving).

By this time, of course, Aunt Gussie lived in some very plush
apartments on Vermont at Seventh or Eighth Street. These were
not only the top apartments of their day—the movie people lived
there also. No better place, then, for the going-away party that
Aunt Gussie had to throw for her dear niece. I know *that* one
lasted all night! Unfortunately, Ernest could not attend. When
he next saw Hazel, she had been through an unfortunate re-
bound marriage and her funds had been quite diminished.

Hazel ended up living with her former in-laws, the Fosters.
Apparently, she was having quite a distressing time of it. Later
on, and shortly after the publication of the 1926 edition of the
Science of Mind textbook, Aunt Gussie showed up one morning
at Ernest's practitioner office with Hazel physically in tow. It
was obvious that there had been words in getting her this far.
"I told her she needs to talk to a practitioner," said Gussie as
she deposited Hazel on Ernest's doorstep.

Fortunately, Ernest had some open time in his schedule.
Always interested in solving the problems of others, he kindly
invited Hazel into the office and closed the door. Normally, he
was able to diagnose a case in fifteen or twenty minutes and
recommend a solution. This time, however, it was nearly an
hour before the door opened.

Hazel's demeanor was entirely different when she came out
from when she went in. "I wasn't aware," she bubbled, "that
Ernest and I had met before. But do you know, he told me I
was the second person he met when he first came to California

53

and landed in Venice many years ago! Isn't that amazing? And he has remembered me all those years!''

Aunt Gussie paid the fee for treatment, took her niece by the arm, and shepherded her out the doorway, all the while listening in wonderment. ''Do you know,'' continued Hazel, ''that man is on such intimate speaking terms with the Father, I'll just bet you he refers to him privately as 'Papa'! You know,'' she looked at Gussie impishly, a mischievous gleam in her eyes, ''I think I'll call *him* 'Papa.' '' Although Ernest was three years Hazel's junior, the name stuck with him—and with her.

Hazel had heard Ernest speak before, either with her mother or with Aunt Gussie, but this was actually the first time she had met the man on a personal basis. Hazel at once threw herself into the work—learning, studying, and listening to Holmes the lecturer and observing Holmes the man.

When, soon after this, the Institute of Religious Science was chartered, Gussie Rundel was a natural to be the Public Relations representative, handling this department from the very beginning. And, since she hadn't given a Valentine's Day party yet, what more fitting way to celebrate the incorporation of the Institute than with a big, *loving* party?

I wondered later if there wasn't a little collusion, perhaps, in that party. Matchmaking was the role Aunt Gussie loved to play to the hilt, and Aunt Annie wasn't above being a co-conspirator. Although she had had Ernest under her wing from the very early days, even down to selecting his clothes and directing his speaking career, she had been unable to make a match for him.

54

Was it possible, I wondered later (viewing these matchmaking sisters with their heads together nodding in satisfaction at the sight of Ernest and Hazel together), that they actually plotted to encourage a relationship that might lead to marriage?

This brings us, then, close to the fateful year of 1927—of great significance to Ernest both personally and in terms of his life-work: Ernest becoming even more himself.

And that was ever Ernest.

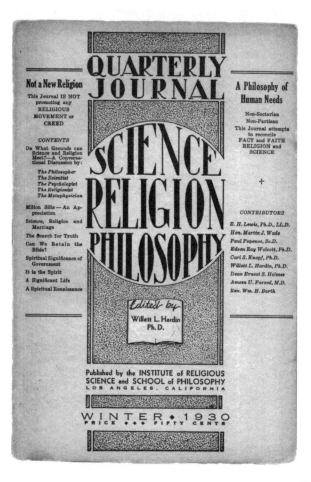

QUARTERLY JOURNAL

SCIENCE RELIGION PHILOSOPHY

Not a New Religion

This Journal IS NOT promoting any RELIGIOUS MOVEMENT or CREED

CONTENTS

On What Grounds can Science and Religion Meet?—A Conversational Discussion by:

The Philosopher
The Scientist
The Psychologist
The Religionist
The Metaphysician

Milton Sills — An Appreciation

Science, Religion and Marriage

The Search for Truth

Can We Retain the Bible?

Spiritual Significance of Government

It is the Spirit

A Significant Life

A Spiritual Renaissance

A Philosophy of Human Needs

Non-Sectarian
Non-Partisan

This Journal attempts to reconcile FACT and FAITH RELIGION and SCIENCE

✝

CONTRIBUTORS

E. H. Lewis, Ph.D., LL.D.
Hon. Martin J. Wade
Paul Popenoe, Sc.D.
Edson Ray Wolcott, Ph.D.
Carl S. Knopf, Ph.D.
Willett L. Hardin, Ph.D.
Dean Ernest S. Holmes
Ameen U. Fareed, M.D.
Rev. Wm. H. Barth

Edited by
Willett L. Hardin
Ph. D.

Published by the INSTITUTE of RELIGIOUS SCIENCE and SCHOOL of PHILOSOPHY
LOS ANGELES, CALIFORNIA

WINTER ♦ 1930
PRICE ♦♦♦ FIFTY CENTS

Chapter 8

♦

WORKS
AND
DAYS

THE STUDY of the Science of Mind is the study of original First Cause, that ultimate Stuff from which all things are made, the Thing itself.'' So spoke Ernest Holmes.

> Man has called It by many names throughout recorded history, but the name is unimportant. Universal principles are not respecters of persons. Heaven has no favorites.

So he spoke when we first met. So he spoke to the day of his departure from this plane of existence. So he spoke in the textbook, *The Science of Mind*. He believed that each person would derive a great good from a sound understanding of the natural laws of life; that they were not to be approached with fear or superstition—with awe, perhaps; but that there certainly is nothing supernatural about the study of life from a metaphysical viewpoint.

To change the race belief from duality to monism, from a belief in good *and* evil to a realization that good is universal and that duality comes from an incorrect use of humankind's power of choice—a choice made in ignorance and resulting in suffering—is the mission of Science of Mind. Humanity's intelligence in this Universal Mind, functioning at the level of each one's concept of it, is of the essence of this teaching. Our approach should therefore be direct, specific, as we begin to accept today more good than we had yesterday. The possibilities are limitless!

This is what he taught.

Ernest was a practical person. "There are too many beautiful theories expounded by too many alleged experts with credentials a mile long, meddling in other people's affairs," he said. "The only trouble is that the theories don't work in practice. Reg, I'd rather have you demonstrate one principle of this science than propose a thousand theories. It's so simple!" Certainly the few principles he began to explore *were* simple. And experience demonstrated their practical nature.

All things change in human experience except the Thing Itself, the Thing that started it all in the first place. Humans change, and the things made by humans crumble. This Thing, by whatever name the individual calls It, is the only reality—God.

Ernest wouldn't call It *God* in the early days. He was a rebel—but a rebel *with* a cause: First Cause.

Know that any form not of the original Harmony is subject to change. We can change conditions in our lives, but it must begin with the individual. The state is only the collective consciousness reflected from individuals; and one with God is a majority.

There are no new words in these statements. He claimed no revelation, no esoteric or occult vision. He said, "This knowledge has always been available to each generation. Some have understood it, some have ignored it."

He felt that the veil between matter and Energy (Spirit) is very thin; that this Universal Energy flows through, in, and around all that is. He explained how anyone can use the Life Energy of the Universe for good. We have already seen the results of its misuse over the ages. It is called the law of cause and effect. Ernest said, "If you don't like the effect you're getting in your life, change the cause." This was the teaching, the wisdom of the ages that came to be pressed between the covers of a book. The book, soon to appear, was *The Science of Mind*.

The last year that the Holmes brothers were together on the platform—1924—he and Fenwicke had started calling the work The Science of Mind—about this elusive Thing that undergirded all that was; this Law that did all things, all ways; this Principle that guided and directed the Law of all good. They had both spoken on the Science of Mind from the platform; but, as we have seen, Fenwicke had gone on to other fields of endeavor.

In 1925, Ernest met his cousin Idella Chadwick in Boston and he told her that a local schoolteacher, Ann Shipman, was taking all his manuscripts and putting them into book form. "It will give us a textbook," he told her, "a teaching textbook at last." And so it was done. The following year, 1926, saw the publication of the textbook, *The Science of Mind*.

That same year, Ernest began speaking each Sunday morning in the theater at the Ambassador Hotel, which seated approximately 600. Within a year, latecomers couldn't get in. The Sunday morning talks were moved in November of 1927 to the Ebell Theatre, which seated 1295. Within a year that also was too small an auditorium.

During the next few years progressive moves were made, one to the beautiful Sala de Oro of the Biltmore Hotel in the heart of Los Angeles; and in 1934 the services were moved to the large Wiltern Theatre at Wilshire and Western boulevards, with a capacity of about 2800. There too, before long, hundreds were turned away every Sunday.

In 1926, far-sighted friends—important men in Los Angeles —had begun to urge Ernest to form a corporation and organize for the inevitable growth of what he was teaching. But Ernest was adamant. "No," he said; "I don't want to do that. I don't want to start a new religion. I don't want to be responsible for a new religion. We have too many religions as it is now." But the subjective pattern was being formed nevertheless.

Unable to budge Ernest, these men came to me privately, and there were long sessions far into the night. They adopted Ernest's own words: "We shouldn't be selfish and keep this just for ourselves. It needs to be given to the world."

"Ernest," I said to him soon after this, "they want to do something for us. We should unify with the biggest ideas we can imagine and realize that ideas govern our power of attraction, and therefore we should constantly enlarge them."

"No, Reg; they are talking about *starting a church*."

But the friends persisted. Didn't he really believe that this teaching was the greatest thing in the world? And, they argued, surely this was something that he thought valuable?

They finally convinced me. And because I wanted a place in the organization, I convinced Ernest that we should become incorporated as a nonprofit religious and educational organization. So a Board of Governors was chosen and a charter was applied for.

In February of 1927, the Institute of Religious Science and School of Philosophy, Incorporated, came into being. Headquarters were established at 2511 Wilshire Bouelvard, covering the entire second floor and comprising business and practitioner offices, as well as a library and lecture hall.

Ernest had resisted the idea of any organization from the start. But now there were seven men in the front office who were living proof of—*organization!* A Board of Governors they were called. Still Ernest would have no part of it: he wanted no position on this Board. "My job," he said, "is to deliver the water of Life, to keep it flowing. Your task is to post the signs showing people where to find it. What we are all trying to do here," said Ernest as he looked around the room at the first Board of Governors meeting, "is 'unscrew the inscrutable.' That's what we're doing with the teaching." Two years after the Institute was founded, Ernest's words reflected some of the accommodation he then brought to the idea of an Institute:

> Regardless of its name or its ultimate purpose, the Institute of Religious Science is a religious institution—a place to which people go to find a satisfaction for that soul-hunger which is inherent in all normal people. That it is, and by its nature it must ever continue to be a substitute for the church which they for the most part left in order to become associated with it.

Nevertheless, those coming through the halls of the Institute for training in the Science of Mind were not infrequently out of harmony with the vocabulary of metaphysics even after our schooling and being out in the field for several years. I recall one time when a group of ministers were discussing holding the ministerial convocation and invited Ernest to attend. They called it the Summer Retreat. Ernest bristled. When queried, he responded, "I won't go! I never want to retreat! But if you'll call it an *advance*, I'll go."

From that moment of shocked surprise, no further retreats were ever discussed, and the annual Asilomar experience is known as our summer *conference*.

The seventh man on that original Board of Governors was myself, Reg Armor. I was also made Secretary of the corporation. It was quite an honor for me to sit in the company of the distinguished and successful men who occupied the six other positions, and I was very proud that my Scoutmaster had seen fit for me to be his representative on the Board—even though he would take no active part in the management of the Institute at this point.

I have written that Ernest, at the beginning, would not take an active part in the management; but I certainly do not wish to imply that he was not active in the affairs of the Institute. Ernest was the central, solar body around which everything in the Institute revolved. It was his determination which way, in which direction, the teaching should go. He just didn't want to be bothered with details. He was not a details man. He wanted to do his "thing," which was to talk about God, the Infinite, the Absolute. This he did, like no individual of my experience, past or present.

It may be that Ernest Holmes will yet "turn on" the whole world, so that each individual has the opportunity to do his "thing" consciously, through the excitation of Creative Mind. This may be the answer to some of the world's problems: instead of being inhibited, the individual should perhaps be excited, thrilled, and joyous to consciously express these qualities of God—Love, Light, Life, Peace, Power, Beauty, Joy—through an unfailing Law of his consciousness. It's no wonder Hazel called Ernest "Papa." He really had a very intimate acquaintance with the Father. He was truly a turned-on individual, combining the fervor of the evangelist with the cold, hard reasoning logic of the research scientist.

Only several months after the establishment of the Institute, a monthly magazine was launched, its title *Religious Science*. The Institute also launched, three years after this, another magazine, the *Quarterly Journal of Science, Religion, and Philosophy*, under the editorship of Dr. Willett Hardin of the University of Southern California, designed to supplement *Religious Science*. An impressive publication, with contributions by distinguished scholars, it was later made over by the Institute to the University of Southern California.

The Institute was not yet equipped to enroll all the would-be students who wanted to attend, so *Religious Science* magazine was created to build and sustain an increasing interest that the Institute had already generated by word of mouth.

In Volume I, Number 1, Ernest announced that as

a semireligious periodical ethical in its tendency, moral in its tone, philosophical in its viewpoint, it will seek to promote that universal consciousness of life which binds all together in one great Whole. . . . It will also be the purpose of *Religious Science* to present to its readers a systematic and comprehensive study of the subtle powers of mind and spirit, in so far as they are now known; and to show how such powers may be consciously used for the betterment of the individual and the race.

And so the magazine *Religious Science* was born, its name changed to *Science of Mind* two years later (1929) to conform with the title of the textbook.

Like so many other ideas of Ernest Holmes, the first issue contained features that have endured. One was a meditation for each day of the month—a one-line meditation at the top of each of 31 of the 32 pages in that first issue. There was also a listing of Religious Science Practitioners—eight names, of which one was Anna Holmes, Ernest's mother.

From the very first issue, the magazine found its way into "learned" circles and so did not go unchallenged by the materialistically inclined. Such a one was a professor at a great southern California university. Shortly after the initial issue, he sat down front at a Sunday night lecture, his Phi Beta Kappa key dangling conspicuously from his watch-chain.

After the lecture, he introduced himself. "Mr. Holmes, your new magazine was quite a topic of discussion following our last faculty meeting," he said. "I firmly believe that the separation of science and religion is just as necessary as the separation of church and state."

"Well, now," said Ernest; "*separation* is a word that we must be very careful of using," and he launched into a post-lecture review of his topic that night, "The Thing Itself."

Some ten or fifteen minutes later, as Ernest paused for breath, the professor baited his semantic trap. "You know, Holmes," he said, "apparently you *do* understand your topic; and if a person could spare a few evenings a week, perhaps he could understand what you are talking about. But let's face it: the research scientist is busy in his ivory tower or his laboratory, and Mr. Average is struggling to make a living. For the thing to be meaningful to the masses of our day, you've got to be able to say *just what it is* in twenty-five words or less. Define your terms. Just what *is* Religious Science, anyway?"

Ernest's eyes gleamed. He took a program out of his coat pocket, turned it over, and extemporaneously jotted down the following: "Religious Science is a correlation of the laws of science, the opinions of philosophy, and the revelations of religion applied to the human needs and the aspirations of man.''

"Deducting the *a*'s and the *the*'s, that's twenty-three words," said the professor, counting. He left impressed, and he later became a staunch friend and booster of my friend Ernest Holmes. And to this day, no one has come up with a better definition of the teaching.

So Ernest now had the teaching between the covers of a book. He had the organization in the form of the Institute of Religious Science and School of Philosophy. And he had his magazine, which was to go out into every state in the union and into more than 75 countries of the world.

No one could perceive in 1927 where the Science of Religion would lead or even what a synthesis of religion and science would be. Perhaps Ernest could.

That would be Ernest.

Chapter 9

♦

ACTIONS
AND
ATTRACTIONS

So by 1927 I was not yet 24 years old, had no college degree, no broad liberal education in the arts or sciences—and here I was sitting on a Board of Trustees, under a State of California charter, with men both learned and successful. As Secretary of the corporation, I kept the records, with nobody commenting when I took notes in longhand. Still, I had one thing in common with these men: we were all religious rebels as far as orthodox creeds were concerned.

And I had been on the "Long March" with Ernest—longer, in fact, than all of these others. Ernest and I shared great emotional compatibility; and the sixteen-year difference between us made him feel very much like a father to me, just as I always felt like one of Ernest's own flesh and blood.

Also, from about the very first time I talked with Ernest,

I felt the desire to be of service to others, to help people—which in terms of Religious Science would mean being a practitioner.

This ambition was realized when I graduated from high school in 1921, just past the age of 18. My very first job as a professional practitioner came several years before the inception of the Institute. At that time Ernest Holmes' headquarters were at Ninth and Grand in Los Angeles. The Trinity Auditorium, which was later renamed the Embassy Hotel, at that time had large rooms behind it in a separate building, with a metal staircase and alleyway between them. As I remember it, we had set up in the North Hall of the Trinity. One corner of the hall had been walled off, open at the top. There we had several little offices, and there it was that I acquired my first actual practitioner experience.

I shared an office with Mother Holmes. We alternated so that there was somebody in attendance each day, where anyone with a problem could come in and talk with a practitioner. Mother Holmes would take three days and I would take three days. Mine were Tuesday, Thursday, and Saturday. Early in my career I found my youth a handicap in counseling with older people, so I grew a mustache when I was fresh out of high school. It not only made me look older but it made me feel wiser.

Ernest would give lectures in the North Hall and then we would hold morning classes. In the afternoon a practitioner would be available to anyone who came in. I must confess that in the early days, my practitioner experience was pretty much like Ernest's. There were days and days when nobody showed up, simply because few were aware that practitioner services were available.

Ernest had several times offered to pay my way through college, but I felt that there were no college courses that could be of value to me, because what I really wanted was to be a practitioner, and there was no place I could learn to be a practitioner other than with Ernest Holmes; so I didn't go to college. At any rate, I actually made my living for several years after this time as a *practicing* professional practitioner.

Within three months after the Institute was chartered, we were discussing larger quarters than the Ambassador Theatre, and in November of 1927 we moved to the Ebell Club Theatre, which seated 1250 people. Ernest always insisted on a simple Sunday lecture. He would permit no flowers beside him on the platform. He wanted nothing to detract from his message.

A month after going to the Ebell Theatre, we decided to put Religious Science on the radio for twelve weeks. The radio program, originated by Ernest and later titled *This Thing Called Life*, aired for many years after his passing, conducted by Dr. William Hornaday, pastor of Founder's Church of Religious Science.

The original intent was for Ernest to give a weekly lesson on Sunday, with Monday through Saturday covered by other speakers, so that each one of us had a particular day of the week. For many years Friday was my day to speak.

The next day, Ernest would greet me coming down the hall and say, "Well, Reg, did you make big talk last night?" After one particularly enthusiastic such burst, he grabbed me by the arms and waltzed me around the room saying,

Talk, talk, talk, talk.
I love its giddy gurgle.
I love its fluent flow.
I love to wind my tongue up.
I love to hear it go.
I used to think I knew I knew,
But now I must confess
The more I know I know,
I know I know the less.

and we burst out in gales of laughter and back-slapping.

Years later I found out from a very learned person that Ernest was actually paraphrasing Socrates' words in Plato's *Phaedrus*. At the time, it seemed only a very, very funny situation, typical of the very human Ernest I knew.

However, Ernest did not particularly enjoy his radio stints. He was a performer, and he loved a live audience. The inner play between speaker and audience always seemed to be thrilling to him, to be rewarding. He would have been in his element in the day of the Earth Satellite beaming sight and sound to a world-wide audience.

From the beginning there was a constant parade of personalities through the Institute doors as Ernest sought for key people to assist in the growth. One of those who crossed his consciousness was Frank B. "Doc" Robinson from Moscow, Idaho—sometimes called "The Mail-Order Prophet."

Doc Robinson had been a druggist who was disillusioned with organized religion. He developed a home-study course called Psychiana, which he widely advertised and sold. In fact, he must have been the J. Walter Thompson of his day, because one could hardly pick up a periodical or a newspaper or a magazine without seeing an advertisement headlined "I talked to God," by Doc Robinson.

It was inevitable, then, that one so widely known, so widely read, should eventually walk through the doors of the Institute. And while Ernest was personally very much impressed with Doc Robinson, the two of them never worked out any permanent arrangement. About the most that ever came of the visits was that Doc Robinson had a joint venture with Ernest whereby they both appeared on the platform at the Philharmonic Auditorium. When Doc Robinson passed away some years later, his work died with him because, despite the tremendous advertising and sales, there was no organization to carry on his work.

It is possible that his passing confirmed Ernest's growing conviction that the works that a person accomplishes in his or her own lifetime may be very great, but when that person passes from the scene, there has to be some sort of organization to carry on for him. This was true in the time of Jesus of Nazareth and it was true in the time of Ernest Holmes. Not being much of an organization man, he probably preferred sitting on the sidelines and watching how things developed. It was not until 1932 that the Dean of the Institute, Ernest Holmes, would recognize the need to participate on the Board of Trustees.

The original Institute charter provided for two classes of membership, like many corporations of its day. The only voting members were the members of the Board; naturally, they sometimes re-elected themselves. All other members were nonvoting members. Despite this self-perpetuating feature of its makeup, the Board's members did not exercise it year after year. But, of course, Ernest's became the premier position on the Board and, as such, remained secure.

1929 was a year of constantly increasing inflation that mounted month by month, week by week. The cost of producing the magazine had risen steadily, whereas income seemed to be going out as fast as, or faster than, it came in. By August, we owed the printer so much that he could foreclose, so it was deemed wise to seek a new printer. Two months later, the bubble of inflated paper credit burst, the banks failed, and the stock market crashed.

When the artificial trappings of the material world are stripped away, people always return to their faith in the Infinite —to that still, quiet center that has never been violated, that has never known hurt, that has never been scarred. And so it was with Religious Science and the Science of Mind. As the economic situation deteriorated over the next few years, the crowds at our Sunday lectures in the beautiful Sala de Oro of the Biltmore Hotel grew and grew. Many friends who had been too busy pyramiding ephemeral profits began to take an interest in the philosophy of the Eternal.

A Sunday program from 1932 indicates that at least this far back, if not earlier, we had many church activities—although Ernest and others around him stubbornly refused to call it a church. In fact, printed right on the program under the *Purpose of the In-*

stitute was the statement that it "is not a church, subscribes to no creed, observes no particular custom, ritual, or performance."

Yet the program shows a church-type service on Sunday, even to the extent of opening with a hymn and having that old post-meditation hymn so familiar to Religious Science churches everywhere, "Open My Eyes." There was always good, professional music, including a prelude by a pianist on this particular day and a violin solo during the offertory.

Also notable are the beginnings of what is now the Ministry of Healing Prayer. It would meet daily at eleven o'clock in the Meditation Room and conduct healing meditation for all who asked for help. There was always an abundance of literature, and the bookroom is a part of every Religious Science center even to this day.

There was something going on almost every day of the week, and a Sunday School, or Junior Institute, was conducted at the Institute headquarters each Sunday at 11:00 A.M., during the time when the Sunday service for adults would be conducted at the Sala de Oro many miles away. The men's and women's clubs, familiar to most church people, were called a Men's Forum and a Women's Forum, and they met at eight o'clock Monday evening. The Women's Forum during these growth years was presided over by Abbot Kinney's daughter-in-law, Mabel Kinney. It boasted 621 members. There was a Bible interpretation class on Tuesday and a service on Wednesday evening for meditation and instruction. This was the forerunner of today's midweek healing services. On Thursdays there was a Mothers' Round Table, and on Fridays at two o'clock there

73

were talks for helping people apply the principles of Religious Science to their everyday lives. Then Friday evenings were devoted to lectures based on the works and teachings of Thomas Troward—so very seminal in Ernest Holmes' formulation of Religious Science. Classes were held three mornings a week, and 150 students were graduated that year from what we then called the Major Course in Religious Science.

If the program stated that the Institute was not a church, the fact is that the Institute performed all the functions of a church from the very beginning and that, like it or not, the organization now existed to spread the teachings of Ernest Holmes to every village and hamlet on the face of the earth.

The persistence of Ernest in asking questions of the Infinite brought him answers—answers to questions that had puzzled mankind throughout many generations. His treatments also brought him abundant supply, for means flow to those who work with the Law. And his happy personality, as well as his spontaneous, uninhibited admitting of no limitation, attracted to him many, many friends.

That certainly was Ernest.

Chapter 10

♦

ROOFS
OVER
MANY
HEADS

NOW THAT Religious Science had found, in the Institute, a "home," the time arrived for Ernest Holmes to have a home of his own. The Holmes house, never a small thing in itself, started getting a little crowded when Fenwicke brought home a new bride from one of his tours, Katherine Eggleston, a staid New Englander—and yet the writer of Wild West stories for magazines! Was there anything these New Englanders couldn't do?

To accommodate family and friends, Ernest had earlier rented a house right on the ocean front at Venice. There, for example, he had as a guest Nona Brooks, one of the cofounders of Divine Science in Denver. There is no certain way of measuring Nona Brooks' influence on Ernest; but perhaps one measure of it is that when, later, it became time for Ernest to acquire his own, increasingly necessary, ministerial credentials, they would be in the Divine Science tradition; and Agnes Galer—the Divine Science minister who was also a sometime member of the Holmes household—would perform the ordination.

Ernest approached the idea of a new home joyously. Typically, it would be more than a place just for himself and his new bride. For one thing, it would be a place where he and the elegant Hazel could entertain to their hearts' content—spacious, comfortable; for increasingly, Ernest was entertaining prominent people.

Ernest's choice fell on the three-and-one-half acres he had bought in 1923 at Palms, a district then outside the Los Angeles city limits. The property was beautiful, with a house sitting atop a hill; and so the entire property came to be known as "The Hill." His marriage to Hazel was the occasion of "moving in." Brother Guy Holmes, always very handy, set to work on remodeling and enlarging the house. He also built another, farther down the hill, for himself, Emma (his wife), and his children.

Still another house was added on subdivided property for Guy's son, Lawrence; and some years later, in 1936, I too moved out to The Hill at Palms with my wife, Helen. From then on we were twice-a-week visitors at the big house on The Hill, more like family than visitors. And when, shortly after my ministerial ordination in 1939, Helen made her transition, I began a four-year period as bachelor father to my young son, which brought me even closer to the Holmeses.

There was always room for more people on the hilltop, and this included Ernest and Hazel's delight in "giving a party," as they expressed it. These sometimes quite spontaneous affairs

ERNEST HOLMES, early 1920s.

VENICE BEACH, 1918. *Standing, l. to r.:* Ernest, Fenwicke, Reginald, Anne Galer. *Seated, l. to r.:* Nona Brooks, Agnes Galer, Letitia Andrews (metaphysical leader, Oakland).

HOLMES RESIDENCE, 3rd Avenue, Los Angeles, 1918. *L. to r.:* Ross Galer, Reginald, Fenwicke (with son, Louis), Ernest (with Guy Holmes' son, Lawrence), Nona Brooks.

ERNEST'S PARENTS, Anna Columbia Heath Holmes and William Holmes, ca. 1900.

Left:
ERNEST, 3rd Avenue residence,
Los Angeles, ca. 1919.

Below:
PANAMA-CALIFORNIA EXPOSITION,
San Diego, 1915. Ernest (*l.*) and
Gussie Rundel (*r.*).

HAZEL HOLMES, 1920s.

ERNEST AND HAZEL, ca. 1950.

REGINALD ARMOR, Venice High School graduation portrait, 1921.

METAPHYSICAL SANITARIUM, 1779 E. Broadway, Long Beach, 1916.

HOLTZCLOUGH STUDIOS, 3251 W. 6th St., Los Angeles: future home
of the Institute of Religious Science.

Above left: HOLMES RESIDENCE (1954-1960), 554 S. Lorraine Blvd, Los Angeles.

Above: LORRAINE BLVD RESIDENCE, view from hallway into den.

Left: LORRAINE BLVD RESIDENCE, living room.

Above:
CAMP HIGH SIERRA,
summer conference,
1953. Lynn and Willis
Kinnear (*l.*), Ernest (*r.*).

Left:
ASILOMAR, 1958.
L. to r.: Elsie and
Reginald Armor, Mark
Carpenter, Ernest.

Above: ASILOMAR, 1954. *L. to r.:* Louise and William Hornaday, Hazel and Ernest, Athena and Jack Fostinis (Vice-Pres., Church of Rel. Science).

Below left: ERNEST, Asilomar, 1954.

Below right: ERNEST, with Raymond Charles Barker, late 1950s.

FOUNDER'S CHURCH, groundbreaking, 1958. *L. to r.:* Norman Van Valkenburgh (Pres., Church of Rel. Science), Ernest, William Hornaday.

FOUNDER'S CHURCH, 1960. William Hornaday, Ernest.

REGINALD ARMOR, 1967.

welcomed people from all walks of life. The Holmeses were just as much at ease with outstanding persons in the business, professional, diplomatic, and creative fields as they were with groups they called "family." Yet to both Ernest and Hazel, people were just people: God-intended beings expressing their divinely individualized selves. If there was one manner that supremely characterized the Holmeses' personality as a couple, it would be that they were always frank and always open. The Holmes house was always open to more and more people, and so was the Holmeses' heart.

Shortly after Ernest and Hazel went to live on The Hill, Hazel's mother came to join them. This was a most unusual situation, having two mothers under one roof; but as Ernest would say laughingly, "There's plenty of room"—just as he said of his philosophy: "It's always open at the top"; and this was the philosophy he both expressed and lived by. "Aunt" Annie Gillan lived with her daughter and Ernest under the same roof until the day she passed on.

Three years after my graduation, the opportunity arose to find myself in the confectionery business. I had never really intended to be anything in life but a practitioner, but the lure was attractive and it was a business that I was familiar with, having put myself through school this way—selling candies, sodas, ice cream, cigars, magazines.

So, together with my brother, I took over the soda fountain at the drugstore where I had worked during my school years. We were successful for a couple of years and had two shops— one in Venice, the other in Santa Monica. Then the Depression struck, and we went out of business—not bankrupt, but with nothing to show for it.

The blessing of the Depression—and a blessing for me it was, although disguised at the time—was that I had found my way back to my first love, from which I had been parted, and that was, and has always been, Religious Science.

Many who have found turbulence in the outer world of effect and turned to the inner source of strength have found their way back to the Father's house. This was true of me. And many who have used the Science of Mind principles have discovered that increased supply has found its way to them. This was certainly true of Ernest during these years.

The growth of the crowds was nothing short of phenomenal. Everywhere he spoke, people came from far and near. Even the stage and backstage were crowded at the lectures. There was a hunger for healing—healing of both body and outer affairs— and Ernest was embarked on a constant search for those who could help him expand.

He knew, personally and intimately, most of the founders of what are now called the Truth movement churches, a number of whom had studied under the Chicago mystic Emma Curtis Hopkins, as had Ernest. To name some: there were Myrtle and Charles Fillmore, founders of Unity, both of whom had had physical healings. There were also Harriet Hale Rix and her sister Annie Rix Militz, cofounders of the Home of Truth churches. And of course there was Nona Brooks and her sisters, she the president of the Divine Science College in Denver. Ernest knew George Burnell and his talented wife, Mary, in the San Gabriel Valley, teachers of *The Axioms of Reason*. He spoke with Fred-

78

erick L. Rawson, the English healer, who wrote the influential textbook *Life Understood*; and there was Dr. Frank Riley, director of the Krotona Theosophical Society, whose pupils became ours too, for the practical application of cosmic law that we taught.

The magazine, which went from being *Religious Science* to *Science of Mind*, at first maintained largely by the generosity of Board member Lem Brunson and a few other persons deeply interested in spreading the good news of Religious Science, grew steadily under the editorship of Maude Allison Lathem, who in later years was succeeded in that post by Willis Kinnear. As for the ''pioneer'' editorial staff, it was composed of Ethel Winton, editor; Josephine Holmes (Guy's daughter and Ernest's niece), assistant editor; and Augusta Rundel and Helen Van Slyke, associate editors.

Meanwhile, we had provided classrooms for teaching a definite school program. In the early years, Ernest Holmes did most of the teaching himself, although we gradually added a teaching staff and expanded the Major Course.

The organized effort and teaching program attracted outstanding people from a broad field of subjects who lectured in our classes. We had such persons as Rabbi Ernest Trattner and Rabbi Ira Magnin as well as outstanding people from the Catholic and other church groups. One such was William Barth, a Congregational minister, who later assumed the duties of Director of Education for several years.

We secured the services of many teachers and professors from the colleges, such as Professor Ralph Flewelling of the School of Philosophy, USC, founder of the review *The Personalist*, and Professor Carl Knopf, Dean of the School of Religion, also of USC, who made archeology come alive with Bible characters through his lectures. And from USC, too, came W. Ballentine Henley, who would later become president of the College of Osteopathic Physicians and Surgeons. Still another who lectured for us in the early days and for many subsequent years was Frederick Woellner, Professor of Education at UCLA; and Ameen Fareed, an outstanding Los Angeles psychiatrist who had practiced in Cairo, Egypt, was one of Ernest's very close friends.

Others who joined our Religious Science teaching staff with training in similar schools of thought were Ernest's cousin Idella Chadwick, Isobel Poulin, Ivy Crane Shelhamer, Clarence Mayer, Robert Bitzer, Elizabeth Murphy, Carmelita Trowbridge, Clarence Flint, and Margaret Wales. They are but a few of the teachers and practitioners who played an important part in those early years.

In time, many others were attracted to the growing organization and made a definite contribution to the growth of the teaching and lecturing program. A few such persons were John Hefferlin, Paul Brunet, Raymond Charles Barker, Elizabeth Carrick-Cook, Frederick Bailes, Dan Custer, Joseph Murphy, Catherine Harris, Lillian Hopper, Wayne Kintner, Stanley Bartlett, and Fletcher Harding. Many of these people later went out into the field and became leaders of activities associated with the Institute. Two such who come to mind were Clifford and Sally Chaffee. Some of the above, like Carmelita Trowbridge, Joseph Murphy, and Frederick Bailes, later established independent activities of their own.

80

There was a constant flow of people through the Institute doors in the early years, and Ernest's explorations often wandered far afield. One night I saw him in one of many serious conversations with Superior Court Judge Ben Lindsey. He had established the very first Juvenile Court in the United States. Seeing the children from broken homes, he advocated not free love but "Companionate Marriage" (the title of one of his books), which today is almost a commonplace.

In 1934 Ernest brought in Dr. Clinton Wunder, a minister who had been assistant to Will Hays, President of the Motion Picture Producers and Distributors of America (1922–45). Dr. Wunder was made co-dean to share Ernest's workload, they shared an office, and they spoke on alternate Sundays. To my knowledge this is the only time that the idea of a co-dean was ever tried. Dr. Wunder's contract was not renewed at the end of the first year—it just didn't work out.

Ernest was very zealous for growth, and he wanted a worldwide organization. Perhaps he was seeking someone just like himself—an alter ego, or a multiplication of himself so that the philosophy could be carried forward in other places just as he had carried it. But no one will ever take the place of Ernest Holmes, and it would be futile for anyone to try. *And why should they?* But this doesn't mean that we can't or won't have outstanding people. Ernest would be the last person to say, "Build this around me," or "around the memory of me."

But multiplication of oneself isn't the way things work. Ernest Holmes was an individualization of the One Mind, just as each of us is. No one can be something that they are not, and no one can be duplicated by another. I can hear him now speaking of another person he had tried to bring into a position of leadership: "That man got on the horse and rode off in all directions."

There was no self-seeking in Ernest's appraisal of himself, no false ego—just a simple statement of fact. "I have no superiors," he said, "and but damn few equals."

That was a fact; and that was Ernest.

Chapter 11

◆

N O
CHURCH(!)

THE MORAL law of the Universe is progress. Every generation that passes idly over the earth without adding to progress
remains uninscribed in the register of humanity. Yet "just poke
your finger in a bucket of water and see how big a hole you
make," Ernest would say, illustrating his deflation of the ego-
self. Religious Science, bigger than Ernest or any other of its
messengers, would nevertheless be a contribution to humanity
that anyone could take part in.

An early article in the magazine under Ernest's signature
says:

The philosophy of Religious Science is nothing new to
the world. It is rather a synthesis of the greatest concepts
which have ever come to the mind of man. The law of
Moses, the love of Christ, the ethics of Buddha, the
morals of Confucius, the deep spiritual realization of the
Hindus, the mystical revelations of the saints of the Middle Ages, the laws of parallels and compensation of Emer-

son, the logic of Kant, the spirituality of Swedenborg, the beauty of Browning, and the wide, universal sweep of Walt Whitman all find an exalted place in the philosophy of Religious Science.

The very name ''Institute of Religious Science and School of Philosophy, Inc.'' indicated the trend of Ernest's thought. At times predating recorded history, the ancient mysteries of Being were taught in schools by a very learned priesthood—a very select and tightly knit group subject to finite error, yet beyond finite question.

In his own experience, Ernest had brothers who were ministers—members of this select group, the ''priesthood,'' who nevertheless could not make a decision without consulting a board of trustees, here again being subject to finite error and finite opinion. Ernest felt, in synthesizing the wisdom of the ages, that he had something better; that each one could go *directly to the source*; that one needed no priesthood or intermediary to intercede on one's behalf or act as ''middleman.'' The Science of Mind concept is rather that each one maintains one's individuality in consciousness and thus each has a ''hotline'' to the Father-Mother. Just as each snowflake is different, each fingerprint is different, each voiceprint is different, each bloodprint is different, so each one of us is an individualization of the One.

Ernest would accept no limitation on his own spontaneous individuality, and to him the word *church* spelled organization and limitation—and he would have none of it. He regarded God-as-Law as being mechanical, the Doer; God-as-Spirit as being spontaneous, the Thinker. He did not place the ministry on a

84

pedestal, nor did he feel that there was anything sacred about the pulpit. Ernest would have no church, nor would he permit any competition with established churches, of which he felt there were already much too many.

If ministers wanted to come to him, well and good. If they wanted to take the teaching and philosophy back to their own churches, excellent! Orthodoxy needed a shot in the arm. Better still, if they wanted to go out and start their own work, using Science of Mind principles, he would help them. This original line of reasoning was not always in accord with the feelings of those of a more orthodox conditioning.

Two years after the establishment of the Institute, in the minutes of the Board of Trustees meeting of February 22, 1929, we find the policy of the organization still under discussion. Ernest's own words, recorded in those minutes, set forth his personal feelings in the matter at that point:

Dean Holmes presented his ideas regarding the policy of the Institute as follows:

"First, that the Institute may be developed as a school of philosophical training from which persons who had received the training might go out to other cities and start centers for which they would be personally responsible and for which the Institute would have no responsibility.

"The work in the centers would follow on the lines of model work conducted by the Institute in Los Angeles. Using this plan, it was explained, there would be no competition with established churches, but rather a

tendency for churches to send specially chosen represen-
tatives to the Institute for training.

"The second plan suggested was that the Institute
train people and send them out under the auspices of the
Institute to establish centers in other localities. Under this
plan, it was explained, the Institute would be responsible for all centers and pay the salaries of the center leaders
and would be in direct competition with churches."

Dean Holmes stated that in his opinion the first plan
would give the work an infinitely broader scope.

In Ernest's search for qualified and competent personnel to
expand the work there was a constant flow of ministers and
educators who could not quite absorb the Holmes line of reasoning. He thought along the lines of the universal and the ecumen-
ical long before these terms became fashionable. So another ten
years would elapse before the Institute would train its first
ministerial class. Ernest was thinking bigger than a church or
a denomination or a religion.

Very early there existed in Ernest's thought a world training
center for the universal Sonship of man, under the universal
parentage of the One, no matter by what name this One was
called, where people of all faiths, all creeds, all colors, all kinds
of speech, all areas of learning could be one in the feeling of oneness that they had with the Infinite.

A clear picture in subjective mind cannot help but materialize its form on the objective side of life. In 1934 the Sala de

Oro room of the Biltmore Hotel was to be closed for remodeling into what became the Biltmore Ballroom.

Ernest's good friend, Rabbi Ernest R. Trattner, the articulate and dapper spiritual leader of the local Reform Jewish Temple Emmanuel, offered Ernest the use of the temple to hold services since their congregation was considering a move to larger quarters. Because the temple did not have the seating capacity of the Biltmore room, it was necessary for us to hold two services.

We tried this out, but two services were just not satisfactory. People did not come and overall attendance fell off. This was our first experience with trying to hold Sunday services in a "church," and although the experiment did not succeed, it nonetheless exemplified the high regard for Ernest in the minds of many ecclesiastical leaders.

So it came about that in June 1934, we moved Sunday services to the Wiltern Theatre, which seated 2800. Here again the success of previous years was repeated, so that it wasn't too long before we were turning away 400–500 people on Sunday. There was just no place to put the crowd that came to hear Ernest during those years. Nevertheless the services continued at the Wiltern for ten years, until the management wanted to show their motion pictures at an earlier hour. Ernest later had a nine-year ministry at the Beverly Hills Theatre; still he would not consider the term *church*.

Shortly after moving services to the Wiltern, we inaugurated a fund for the purchase of a world headquarters building should one become available that suited Dean Holmes' plans.

One day, a year later, Gussie Rundel charged breathlessly into headquarters. "I've found it! I've found it!" she said.

"Found what?" asked Ernest. "I didn't know 'it' had been lost!"

"Oh, *I've found it!*" said Gussie. "I've found our headquarters. Our world headquarters!"

At this statement all ears opened up and every eye was focused on Gussie.

"The building over near my apartment," exclaimed Gussie, her eyes shining. "Holtzclough!"

I looked at Ernest. Ernest looked at me.

"Holtz Cloe?" we questioned.

"What's a Holtz Cloe?" I asked.

"No, no," said Gussie. "It's not *what's* a Holtzclough. It's *who's* a Holtzclough."

Holtzclough was the leading interior designer in the city. "He's considered, by everyone that knows, to be the best—and this building says as much. There are three floors, and it's just a beautiful spot!" she enthused.

We hastened to see this beautiful spot of Gussie's, and truly she had not exaggerated. At the time we first saw our International Headquarters building there were springs flowing down behind it; cottages across the street; and where there is today the superstructure of an office building, there was just an arroyo wash. In time, this lovely Institute building was completely surrounded by the city. We were "in the world but (still) not of it."

Although the building was relatively new when we first beheld it, the décor was in the manner of Europe centuries past.

It had a feeling of antiquity, durability, and stability—a little bit of the Old World set down in the midst of the New. Let Gussie Rundel tell you about it, 24 years later, for our first impression of it was the same as what she set down in 1959:

> As we walked down the hallway for the first time, our thoughts were in unison. *This building had been built for the Institute.* The dean's office at Headquarters had been office number three, and Ernest walked back to the third office, opened the door with the same air of Columbus discovering America, gazed around the venetian-paneled room, sat down behind the elaborate desk, and said, ''It's mine.''
>
> He claimed it just like Columbus setting down his staff on the New World. This was to be Ernest's new world.
>
> Coming back down the hallway, I opened the door of the first office, which we looked in. It had been paneled with walls taken down from an old English manor house, and I sat down at the desk and said, ''It's for me.''

So, like the three bears claiming their chairs and porridge, we each laid claim to our particular niche at world headquarters. The office that I have always occupied is the same office that I claimed for myself at that time.

There was no time lost in finalizing the move. Holtzclough needed funds and we had the funds. So a meeting of the minds was achieved, and we moved into our world headquarters—3251

W. Sixth Street, Los Angeles. Extensive property was added to the purchase, providing for future expansion. Meanwhile, we completed the alterations at headquarters necessary for converting the workshops and display rooms of the interior designer into classrooms, a library, magazine and business offices, and offices for many staff practitioners.

After the move to a new headquarters in 1935, the germ of the idea was freeing itself and growing. It was perfectly demonstrating at that time the thought Ernest so often expressed in his teaching:

> A thought or an idea is like a seed and has contained within it all the mechanics, lesser ideas, and potential activity to produce the idea involved in it. The only thing we must do is plant it, nurture it, and let it alone to grow.

And if Ernest's speaking had earlier sparkled, now it stood out like a jewel on a black velvet cloth.

1935 was indeed a banner year for Religious Science as interest caught on like a prairie fire. We were gradually building up a representative number of books dealing with the teaching and practice of Religious Science. When the Institute was first chartered, eight years before, we started with three books of Ernest's and six of Thomas Troward's—and there were several of Fenwicke's.

But by 1935 people such as Clarence Mayer, Alberta Smith, and Margaret Wales were among the contributors establishing a distinctive Religious Science literature. Ernest himself had added to the list two books, a booklet, and two books co-authored. Over the years I too would write several books having a steady distribution. These were titled *Very Present Help*, *Mind Does It*, *Thought Is Power*, and *The Magic of Love*.

In later years, such outstanding Religious Scientists as William Hornaday, Lornie Grinton, Craig Carter, Orrin Moen, Lillian Hopper, Wayne Kintner, Raymond Charles Barker, Paul Martin Brunet, Gene Emmet Clark wrote books which contributed greatly to the literature. Ernest always urged that such books be written, and he often co-authored books with others. As he put it, ''Any organization such as ours needs an increasing literary output to go with it.''

I personally feel that, whether he knew it or not, Ernest was ensuring that he would not be put on a pedestal and set apart as the founder of Religious Science; for if there was one thing he did not want, it was being put on a pedestal. This he would not have—just as he would have no church in the early years.

With the establishment of headquarters there ensued great expansion of the teaching. In fact, the following decade, from 1935 to 1945, was the period of greatest growth. In keeping with Dean Holmes' ideas for a world training center, the Institute was reincorporated and the word *School* eliminated. We became the Institute of Religious Science and Philosophy, and we added a Department of Education to expand the teaching.

Expansion was the order of the day in this period. Psychologist Dan Custer of our Riverside chapter promoted a Science of Mind Radio Club from San Francisco in the north to San

Diego in the south and followed this up with a Science of Mind newspaper. The Institute at this time had about 2000 members; we were getting two thousand letters a month, which had to be answered personally; and it was estimated that we were teaching a total radio audience of 40,000 listeners daily.

By the mid-1940s, the Institute was almost paid for. Ernest now agreed to build an auditorium large enough to seat 2000 people. With the onset of World War II, building construction had come to a halt by government decree. But by 1944 we were already looking forward to further expansion at war's end. Religious Science pioneer Clarence Mayer said:

> The various theatres have been lovely, but fundamentally and always they will be just that—theatres. And the vibration that could only be found there is namely one of amusement, something desirable and necessary in our lives but more or less fleeting. Whenever we enter an Episcopal or Catholic church edifice, we feel at once a vibration or atmosphere of reverence, harmony, and peace, because these auditoriums are never used for anything but a worship service. Naturally, we feel a vibration of prayer and uplift, as every building has its own atmosphere or vibration. Let's build a home for Holmes!

In a talk given on September 15, 1944, Ernest said, "We have come for the first time to discuss permanent plans for the erection of our own building for our Sunday morning conference." He still wouldn't call it a Sunday morning *church service*. But he *was* speaking, at last, of an auditorium to be owned by the Institute, seating 2000 people. Twenty-five thousand dollars was enthusiastically subscribed in one hour, with a half-million targeted; but it would be another sixteen years before Founder's Church was dedicated.

Ernest called God, or whatever It is, First Cause—"This Thing called Life"—and he said that each of us is an individualized center *in* It without being an individual *separate from* It. Later on, Ernest expressed the belief that each of our churches was an individualized center in the one church of Religious Science, not an individual church separate from the one. He repeated time and again that there is only one church of Religious Science. From the outset, he saw this wedding of science and religion as *already* established, available to all, firm and prosperous—and *already* functioning as a central headquarters, with a family of affiliated branches. And what he saw is what he demonstrated.

That was Ernest.

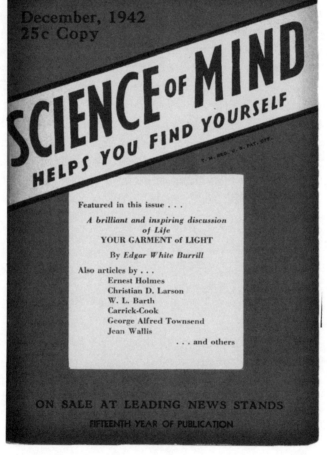

December, 1942
25c Copy

SCIENCE OF MIND
HELPS YOU FIND YOURSELF

T. M. REG. U. S. PAT. OFF.

Featured in this issue . . .

A brilliant and inspiring discussion of Life
YOUR GARMENT of LIGHT

By *Edgar White Burrill*

Also articles by . . .
Ernest Holmes
Christian D. Larson
W. L. Barth
Carrick-Cook
George Alfred Townsend
Jean Wallis
. . . and others

ON SALE AT LEADING NEWS STANDS

FIFTEENTH YEAR OF PUBLICATION

Chapter 12

♦

THEIRS WAS THE PRACTICE

I<small>N ALL</small> times, in all cultures, there have been persons who have performed 'healings' by many means. Ernest Holmes said:

> We have no objection to any form of healing. Any method producing results has its place in the whole. Anything that helps to overcome human suffering is good, whether it be in the form of a pill or a scientific mental realization. God in man as man is man. We do not deny the reality of the human body or the reality of the visible universe. The energies and the laws of nature have been progressively revealed to the human mind as man has been able to comprehend, at his level of awareness, and use these natural laws constructively.

This explains the fundamental differences between Christian Science, formalized as a church over a hundred years ago, and Religious Science, more recently established as a church continuously "open at the top" for new discoveries.

As a matter of fact, Ernest said that a practitioner is an adventurer on the last frontier, the almost unexplored area of Absolute Cause. We know what the Thing is, we know how It works, and we now understand how to let It work for us. We are over the threshold of a new Golden Age of humankind. We control conditions within our own immediate lives, rather than being controlled by outside circumstances over which we have no say. And this has become the feeling and the impulsion of the age.

Ernest also said:

Of course, we believe in all churches and in any form of worship, for above all we certainly believe in a Power for good in the Universe, instantly available to all who know how to use it correctly (righteousness = right use-ness). No one will ever have a complete understanding of the "Truth," and we repudiate any superstition which says that all the Truth has been given. Each orthodox religion has claimed to have the Truth. Yet the actual Truth may be so vast that no one of them could have more than just a mere decimal of the Truth.

Ernest Holmes, having asked questions and received answers as the first Religious Scientist, became its first practitioner. Seeing how Ernest applied Religious Science to his own problems, his cousin Idella Chadwick, visiting the Holmes household a year before the textbook was completed, was impressed.

"Ernest," she said, saying to him what has been said many times by many people, "you've got what I've been looking for all my life. With a teaching background, I've already learned the science of mathematics, chemistry, and physics; and since you call this a science, I can learn it. Of course, if you had called it a religion, I would have run like the dickens. But Religious Science I can learn."

Ernest taught the first courses himself. Later the work was augmented by various teachers as well by guests on correlative subjects. The courses were given both in the daytime and at night. The subject matter covered was the same, but the number of hours varied somewhat between day and night sessions. Upon the successful completion of this one-year program, the student received a certificate as a "Major Student" of Religious Science.

Since at that time we had no credentialing system, those students who so desired called themselves practitioners of Religious Science. They devoted part or all of their time to the mental and spiritual treatment of others. As the classwork continued to grow, more and more of these Major Students were being graduated. Consequently, more and more of them were calling themselves practitioners of Religious Science. Yet many of them had other occupations, and their practitioner work was in the nature of a sideline, just as I myself, in the early 1930s, had my business *and* my practice.

Most of these people were sincere and dedicated to the profession of helping others. However, now and then there were those who thought the whole idea was a scheme that would enable them to enhance their prestige and line their purse. Unfortunately, some of them introduced ideas that were quite foreign to the teaching and practice of Religious Science.

This led to the advisability of issuing credentials in the form of licenses to those who desired to be professional practitioners in the name, and with the blessing, of Religious Science. The reason for this was that there was no regulatory agency governing the activities of spiritual-mind practitioners. The Constitution of the United States guarantees freedom of worship and the practice of religion as long as they entail no fraud or harm. Under this freedom it becomes incumbent upon each religious organization to protect and, in a sense, to supervise those workers who function under its banner.

The Institute, originally chartered as a nonprofit religious corporation, embodied in its corporate structure a provision for recognizing teachers and practitioners as well as elevating qualified persons to the ministry. At a meeting on August 11, 1932, the Board of Trustees had authorized Practitioner, Teacher, and Leader designations, setting forth the requirements to be met for each; but the actual issuance of such recognition had never been established.

By 1939, we felt it necessary to credential our workers. This would help stem the numbers of those who could bring criticism on the name of Religious Science. Imagine practitioners analyzing problems and prognosticating on the basis of the numerological value of a name or from handwriting specimens or the spread of a deck of Tarot cards!

We heard of a practitioner in San Francisco who would say to a client, ''Now if you will give me your exact birthdate, natal hour, etc., I'll work with an expert who will cast your horoscope. This way we will know how to work more intelligently on this situation for you.''

We received reports of another practitioner operating in a very nice tearoom in Hollywood. While a patron was lunching, this very presentable person would approach her saying, ''If you'd just turn your teacup over and turn it around three times, I'll read your fortune for you.'' The fortune having been read, the practitioner would say, ''Now if you ever need any help at all, please call on me'' while offering a business card bearing the designation *Practitioner of Religious Science.*

Upon hearing of these incidents, Ernest would say, ''Well, it's very interesting to have your fortune told or your horoscope cast or to attend séances. But let's face it, Reg, that is *not* the teaching.''

It was therefore with these problems in mind that Clarence Mayer, Idella Chadwick, and I approached Ernest with a plan to initiate an additional course of study, beyond our Major Course work, designed to benefit those wanting to practice professionally under our banner. The three of us had talked the matter over thoroughly and had outlined a schedule of work consisting largely of specific case histories and actual demonstrations of practitioner-patient interviews and treatment work.

We believed that if this were done properly, it would take the place of the three or four years of actual experience we had

99

gone through in setting up our practice—and we also believed that actual practice could minimize the worry about whether anyone would come to us as well as the further worry about what we should do when they *did* come.

When we outlined our plan to Ernest, he said, "That's a wonderful idea! It has my blessing. Let's do it. If they know the teaching, let them demonstrate it to you."

Idella outlined a method giving the individual applicant's statement of the case, what the doctor's diagnosis was, the practitioner's diagnosis, and the kind of treatment he or she gave. All this had to be written out, including what the result was, so that by the time the students were finished with those classes, we could really tell which ones knew the teaching and practiced it. This was the beginning of what we then called the Practitioners' Clinic. Most of the ideas evolved in that first Clinic would remain embodied in that part of our educational program later called the Practitioners' Professional Training course (PPT).

Thus the actual Practitioner, Teacher, and Leader designations, authorized in 1932, were finally made available seven years later. It became necessary for a candidate to be not only a Major Course student but a graduate of the Clinic class before he or she could apply for a license as a practitioner of Religious Science. After satisfactorily completing the application requirements, the candidate was given a practitioner's certificate, or license, which implied the blessing of the organization.

Since these licenses had to be renewed periodically, it can be seen that provision was made in this system for the protection of the organization and its teachings as well as for the protection of the client, who could visit the practitioner with confidence, knowing that all was in order. The system put matters on a more professional standing and was long overdue.

So it was that in 1939 we created policy, procedures, and ethical standards for our first licensed practitioners. It was also in 1939 that we ordained our first ministers of Religious Science. Ernest Holmes and I were members of that first group to receive ordination. Others of that original group were Isobel Poulin, Ivy Crane Shelhamer, and William Barth.

In later years, the scholastic requirements for students and those seeking professional recognition were progressively increased, until today each practitioner has a college education or its equivalent. Also, a ministerial candidate has first to become a practitioner as part of his or her ministerial training.

Someone who is emotionally involved with his or her own problem needs a practitioner. Even a *practitioner* needs a practitioner at times. Idella Chadwick was Ernest's practitioner in the early days; and he would work for her when she had a problem. After Ernest's marriage to Hazel, she became his practitioner, just as he had been hers.

Ernest told his practitioners, upon their graduation, "Now go out and heal. Do the thing. Be the thing itself." He wanted lots of practitioners. "Don't worry about being a success," he said. "Wherever you have an audience, if there is one person healed of a problem, people will flock to your doorstep, so great is the need. This is the way the church will grow." (This was in the mid-1950s, by which time he enthusiastically endorsed the concept of church in order to spread the teaching.)

Spiritual healing is the vitality of our organization. We *should* be "purists," ignoring critics and detractors, staying "at home" with First Cause, which heals. Our physical body and the "body" of our affairs only reflect the inner spiritual realization (or its absence). Inner peace and harmony produce a constant sufficiency of supply, for the Thing that gave you life knows how to sustain and maintain it abundantly.

The practitioner says, with the most perfect practitioner who ever lived, Jesus of Nazareth, "It is not I who do the work. It is the Father within." The practitioner learns to live very close to the Source.

Every practitioner understands these words of Ernest's:

We are always specializing the law of cause and effect for some purpose. Mostly we are doing this unconsciously. Now we must learn to bring our thoughts and purposes into line with the original harmony. In doing this we should not be afraid that we are usurping the divine Will any more than a farmer would be afraid that he is going contrary to the laws of nature or the will of God when he decides to plant corn instead of cotton.

The necessity of choosing is ordained by the very nature of our being and we cannot escape it. We are at liberty to choose what manner of life we shall live. We should feel that in this choice, backed by all the will, all the purpose, and all the law of the Universe, our reliance is on this law and order. It is the creative agency of all life; and at the same time our use of it is personal and individual. Here is all the freedom one could ask for and all the freedom that Divine Mind Itself could have possibly given us—the freedom to act as an individual, the freedom to give full reign to our creative imagination, and the freedom to do this (at least temporarily) in such a way as to produce discord instead of harmony—but also, and what is more important, the freedom to produce harmony instead of discord.

More exciting than outer space, we have crossed the threshold of a new frontier: inner space—the realm of the practitioner.

That was Ernest's dream.

INSTITUTE OF RELIGIOUS SCIENCE

3251 W. 6th St.
Los Angeles 5,
California

CALENDAR
OF MEETINGS
JANUARY
1945

SUNDAY MORNING

AT 11:00 A.M.

ERNEST HOLMES

AT THE WILSHIRE EBELL THEATRE
Corner Wilshire and Lucerne

•

FREDERICK BAILES

AT THE FRIDAY MORNING CLUB'S
TIMES THEATRE
938 South Figueroa

Subjects at Both Services:

Jan. 7—Your God Power
Jan. 14—The Way Your God Power Works
Jan. 21—What Your God Power Does
Jan. 28—How to Use Your God Power

DOXOLOGY AND BENEDICTION

Praise God that good is everywhere
Praise to the love we all may share.
The life that thrills in you and me;
Praise to the Truth that sets us free.

Chapter 13

♦

RELIGIOUS SCIENCE COMES OF AGE

THOMAS ALVA EDISON once said, "A great institution is but the lengthened shadow of a single man." The United Church of Religious Science is certainly the lengthened shadow of Ernest Holmes.

The years 1934 to 1944 were a period when the nations of the world resumed what the politicians in 1918 had called the war to end all wars. However, the turbulence and unrest in the outer world left Ernest untouched. The seed he had planted in mind many years ago had borne fruit. Now was the period of greatest growth. These same ten years at the Wiltern Theatre, which seated 2800 people (including a tremendous balcony), saw each week literally hundreds of people turned away—200, 300, 400, 500 people crowding to get in, with just no place to seat them. Further expansion was clearly needed—but first it would begin within the organization.

In 1938, the Board authorized a fund to provide land and buildings for a central chapter of the Institute, another fund to organize and administer new chapters, an educational fund for training young leaders (whence the licensing of practitioners and ministers the following year), a literature fund for the promotion of writings and writers, and an endowment fund for designated purposes.

Eight years previously, in 1930, Robert H. Bitzer had come from Boston and founded the first branch of the Institute at the Roosevelt Hotel in Hollywood. Although the funds had been authorized, there was no money to back them up at the time; but one aspect of this growing period was the fact that several persons had come to us saying, "I am going to start a branch of your work."

When it was explained to them that there was as yet no provision for branches and that the Board of Trustees was not yet ready to fund their establishment, this did not diminish their enthusiasm and determination. They would reply, "Well, I'm going to start a Religious Science activity whether you call it a branch or not."

It was this persistence that led to the approval by the organization for such groups and activities to be chartered as *chapters* of the Institute, the name of each activity to be "Institute of Religious Science, such-and-such chapter." Each chapter was to be headed by a speaker and was authorized to teach the first-year course in the Science of Mind. Ernest himself often went to places that had made inquiry and would give a series of lectures that stimulated interest in Religious Science in those localities.

In this connection it is both interesting and important to note

106

that in 1932, in view of the growing interest in branch activity, Ernest insisted, with the Board's concurrence, "that any branch must use *The Science of Mind* as its official textbook."

Branch leaders and teachers were to confine their instruction to fundamentals of the teaching. They were not to teach or train others for leadership or teaching roles. That responsibility was reserved to the Institute.

At this point, of course, the term *church* was never used—nor was the leader designated as a minister. They were *chapters* or *associations*, and the leader was the *speaker*. In these activities we could see the vitality of the teaching growing, even faster at times than the organization was prepared to handle. Ernest himself started several chapters, one of which was in Pasadena. Harold E. Gerrard went to San Diego and started another. Ivy Crane Shelhamer, a practitioner, organized a chapter at one of the theaters on Wilshire Boulevard. By the end of 1939 there were five chapters in Los Angeles and eight in other California cities, as well as five affiliated organizations, associations, or "spontaneous" study-groups not necessarily headed by a speaker.

Maude Allison Lathem, a noted magazine editor, helped Ernest revise the *Science of Mind* textbook in 1938, the principal revision being that the chapter on psychic phenomena was deleted, because, as Ernest said, "There is just no way that we can prove these things." Maude's loving assistance in this matter rewarded her with the editorship of the magazine, which she conducted very efficiently over many years, until another great editor, Willis Kinnear, took over.

On March 19, 1940, the first chapter charter was approved for the Hollywood group, with Robert Bitzer as speaker. The

Alhambra chapter was chartered in October 1942, Carmelita Trowbridge the speaker. Huntington Park (Kay Mullendore) soon followed. Other chapter charters granted in this fast-expanding field movement were Pasadena, July 1942 (Elizabeth Larson); Santa Barbara, September 1942 (Thomas Baird); Riverside, September 1942 (Dan Custer); Santa Ana, September 1942 (John Hefferlin); San Diego, July 1942 (Harold Gerrard). The earliest study-group association indicated by our records was the Highland Park group, granted a charter in May 1941.

In time we found that the teaching program of the Institute was forced to expand, each of the chartered chapters now authorized as a teaching chapter of the Institute to conduct the training program for students. Later on some of the teaching chapters were authorized to conduct graduate work in certain districts.

Any organization that experiences rapid growth must also experience some growing pains, and these we did have. There were interested persons from similar activities who were eager to join our organization in some capacity. Needless to say, some of these people were more qualified than others. Some just wanted to be on the bandwagon of success, it seemed, purely for the ride. There were times when Ernest would admit, out of the bigness of his soul, that he had been taken in, and there were times when he admitted to me privately that both he and the organization had been taken advantage of.

There were occasions when I seemed to intuitively perceive that certain persons were not wholly sincere and wanted to join us solely for their own advantage. At such times I would point this out to Ernest and he would listen carefully, frown, and say,

"Perhaps you're right," and then discourage the affiliation. At other times he would refuse to believe that any person in his organization would or could put up a false front.

This is as close as Ernest and I ever came to having disagreements in our relationship. In all our forty-five years of friendship, we never had a serious or lasting disagreement; and on the occasions when he felt his judgment was vindicated, I would give in, for I always respected the fact that Ernest was the founder of the organization and as such deserved the respect due such a person. Then he would playfully dig me in the ribs and say, "Reg—*Reginald*—you're old English!" or "old conservative." This was in reference to my English ancestry and to the fact that I have never believed in snap judgments or first impressions. Too often I have found that these were in error.

At other times, Ernest would jokingly remark to someone, "Reginald is the fellow who pours cold water on things." Given his characteristic enthusiasm, I'm sure he often wondered why I did not share it for certain individuals or certain situations. However, in retrospect I can see that I was right enough of the time to have him respect my sincerity and, to some extent, my frankness in speaking out and voicing my intuition concerning certain persons and situations.

Ernest always had an inner circle, a special group of dedicated workers who met with him each week. Admittance to this group was by invitation only, and we all worked with him on special projects. In Ernest's own words, this activity was one which was most satisfying, as he could let his hair down—he could rise to heights and come back down again, knowing that he would not be misunderstood. And Hazel, who always sat at the rear of the room, would now and then say in a loud voice, "Now, Papa—you know that isn't right" if she thought he had gone a little too far. On such occasions Ernest might come back with some humorous comment, retrace his steps, and get at the subject under discussion from a slightly different angle.

So through the years we have had challenges to meet and problems to solve—as would be the case in any organization, with the problems of each unique to that particular organization. One reason for this in our case is that we never tried to copy or base our organizational structure on any similar-type activity. We learned by experience and made changes as the need arose and as we continued to grow.

In some ways, perhaps, this was a handicap; but in other ways it was carrying out the feeling Ernest had about organized effort. He used to say, "We don't need another religion or just another church. We have, no doubt, too many now." He felt that our teaching and organization should make its unique contribution in the lives and thinking of those who turned to it; and he continued to resist the stifling of any individual's initiative and enthusiasm by insistence on too much organization.

Although it wasn't planned that way, the Institute was nevertheless moving away from the purely "esoteric school" idea, and the idea of *church* was beginning to take hold. This was due largely to the insistence of the leaders of the field activities (many of whom had been ministers in other denominations), and not necessarily to the thinking of headquarters at this time.

As new chapters were chartered and these leaders were ordained in other metaphysical organizations, it was only logical

110

that many of these persons began to think and speak of their chapters as *churches* of Religious Science. They would say, "We are, to all intents and purposes, conducting the activities of a church, so we are going to call our chapter a church."

This idea was not readily accepted by all in the official family, including Ernest. They did not, however, object too strenuously—or perhaps I should say *strenuously enough*, for there was no provision in the organization for such action on the part of any chapter. This development, however, did indicate the trend taking place in the Religious Science movement, and it foreshadowed coming events that later seemed inevitable. It is my personal belief, and one that I think was held by Ernest Holmes at the time, that what was happening was the logical result of the seeds he had planted in the days prior to 1927. There was a new concept of the meaning of church taking place that was attractive and acceptable to those believing in and practicing the teaching of Religious Science.

Easter Sunday of 1943 came on April 23, a day I shall never forget. From the moment Elsie came into my life at a church youth meeting, I knew that I would marry her. My first marriage had been solemnized at Fenwicke's little church in Venice. William Barth, the officiating minister, was one of several ministers who by this time had succeeded him.

Ernest said that when we were ready, he would officiate at a big ceremony on the stage at the Wiltern. Imagine, then, Ernest's surprise when Elsie and I came to the service that Easter Sunday morning breathless and wide-eyed, saying that we had been married earlier that morning by his brother Jerome. Sur-

111

prised he was—but, magnanimous person that he was, he immediately gave us his blessing and joyfully presented us to the congregation before he would allow the service to continue.

We received a jolt when, early in 1944, the Wiltern Theatre management wanted to start showing movies earlier on Sunday. Everyone at the Institute was disturbed by the interference this posed to the Sunday morning service; and there was no auditorium with a capacity greater than the Wiltern's. In fact, most auditoriums had but a fraction of the Wiltern capacity. Ernest typically stuck his jaw out, saying, "I have learned to add but I have never learned to subtract. I will multiply my efforts but never divide them." So on April 7, the Board authorized moving the Sunday service and dividing it between three places.

Stanley Bartlett, a Divine Science minister from Seattle, who then headed the Department of Education, took the outlet at the Friday Morning Club Theatre at First and Vermont. Though this was smaller than the Ebell Club Theatre, it was adequate for the time.

J. Lowery Fendrich, formerly a Presbyterian minister in Washington, D.C., took the outlet at the Wilshire Theatre; and Ernest reluctantly returned to the Ebell Club Theatre, which was overflowing and bursting at the seams wtih people. Never satisfied there, in 1947 he moved to the Beverly Hills Theatre, where he held forth for nine years.

When Ernest decided that he had earned semi-retirement, he turned this outlet over to Gene Emmet Clark, who presided at Beverly Hills from 1956 to 1969. At the time Ernest went to

Beverly Hills, he insisted on my going with him, and our three earlier Sunday morning outlets were then served by Lowery Fendrich, Dan Custer, and Frederick Bailes, a minister from Long Beach, who had healed himself of diabetes, in the years before insulin was readily available, by using the techniques of the Science of Mind.

Fendrich, in September 1946, had come up with the brain-child of a National College of Religious Science, conferring a Bachelor of Religious Science degree for the first-year work. In 1947 he added the Master's degree for the second-year work; and in the following year he added the Doctor of Religious Science degree for a third year of study.

By mid-century, many thousands of people had been through our first-, second- and third-year classes, and in 1950 we under-took condensed and intensive training for both practitioners and ministers. That year the accelerated Ministers' course took twelve weeks to complete, and the accelerated Practitioners' Course was turned out in two weeks of highly intensive training—a policy continued through 1969.

So we had operating "churches" of Religious Science and "churches" of the Science of Mind—but there was no really central, organized *Church of Religious Science*. We had a field department and a field director, and we had an unofficial ministerial association with monthly meetings being held; but no *Church*.

In 1948 Ernest had begun thinking in terms of an expansion department—a world outreach—and in January 1949 he first proposed an International Association of Religious Science

113

Churches (IARSC), and the ministerial association urged him to activate it. Perhaps they somewhat forced his hand to finally accept that Religious Science had come of age. As for the IARSC, it would later pose a delicate problem, yet another with which Ernest and Religious Science would have to deal.

Meanwhile, "Church" was waiting in the wings. Just as surely as government taxation had killed Chautauqua earlier in the century, so did increasing taxation burden the Institute increasingly. But funds that were going for taxation could better be used in spreading the teaching, and so the decision was made to put the Institute into Church form.

Ernest never looked back. He said:

> Religious Science has come of age. It has established a subjective identity in Mind which will carry it forward by its own momentum. There is nothing on the outside which can destroy it. If anything retards its growth, it will be from within—not from without.

Ernest would disclaim any gift of prophecy—yet these words were to prove prophetic.

In 1958 he added:

> We have launched a movement which will be the next new impulsion of modern times, far exceeding in its capacity to envelop the world anything that has happened. We have to have the same faith in what we teach and practice as the scientist has, or the gardener has, and

when that great simplicity shall have plumbed and pene-
trated this density of ours—this human stolidness and
stupidity, this debauchery of the intellect and the soul—
something new and wonderful will happen. It is the only
thing that will keep the world from destroying itself.

That was Ernest's conviction.

Science of Mind

February, 1947   Twentieth Year   25 *Cents*

Chapter 14

♦

REORGANIZATION

ERNEST'S MIND was always open to new ideas. He could discuss anything with anyone—professors of philosophy, psychology, comparative religion; research scientists or physicists; and "the man in the street." In gaining many lifelong friends in various fields, he was respected by one and all for his persistency in searching. However, once convinced that he had found the answer, it was impossible to shake him loose from his conviction. But as the organization grew, there were those who tried.

The horizontal and vertical holds of Ernest's mind-picture of the Institute never wavered. He said many times, "There is only one Institute of Religious Science." Duality in any circumstance was beyond his comprehension. He spoke his word and expected the Law to act on it. He recognized that we have free will to act contrary to Infinite Decree—and that this duality of thought and action creates problems.

After Dean Holmes' opening speech on September 20th, 1944, at the Institute's Alumni Hall, endorsing the idea of a permanent auditorium to be built at war's end, he was followed on the platform by the Institute Business Manager, Bill Haughey, then Chairman of the Board. As enthusiasm mounted, Fred

Bailes sounded what Publicity Director Dan Custer referred to as "the theme of the Tune of Progress being sung by all." Bailes' oratory was fluent—some said it rivaled Ernest's. Fred was then the Institute's principal teacher, and his words resounded through the hall:

> What we are working for is that that great unseen invisible Institute of Religious Science which is everywhere in the hearts of men shall find itself taking form at every point in the universe.

I could see Ernest nodding assent.

But Bailes continued: "I like to think of this prospective building; but in a sense I laugh, because I say, let's get this thing out of the way and get a new one in Chicago—London—Paris."

Ernest's face went blank.

Ten years later, the building had still not been built. The church "home for Holmes" did not quite fit into the founder's mind-model yet. But the church, as such, pursued him.

Meanwhile, the deanery, which the Institute had purchased for their dean's town residence, was desired as a site for a Lutheran church three years after he moved into it. Ernest was reluctant to move out: the convenience suited him just fine. He finally acquiesced only when the Board found him one of the city's fine old mansions, just three blocks away at Sixth and Lorraine, and agreed never to mortgage or encumber it.

As the legal change from Institute status to Church status was being contemplated (finally ratified in 1953), he insisted on writing into the contract a lifetime tenure for himself and for those who had helped set up his first Practitioners' Clinic—Idella Chadwick and me. "Reg," he said, "we had practitioners before we had ministers." And he added:

> The history of all churches is one of eventual tight control by the priesthood. In my own family, I see ministers come and go. If we're going to have a Church, it will be a different Church—and our practitioners make this difference. *The teaching's the thing. Keep the teaching pure.* When we go to a twenty-man board, the number-one spot will be mine by right of consciousness in perpetuity; and *you've* certainly earned a job for life.

When the permanent auditorium was first proposed (1944), Glendale, San Diego, and San Francisco were solid centers for the teaching in the West; the East Coast was represented exclusively by Buffalo, New York.

By the year of the founding of the International Association (1949)—also the year in which Mother Holmes, at the ripe old age of 99, made her transition—there were active operations in Arizona, California, Colorado, Idaho, Minnesota, New York, Ohio, Oregon, Texas, Washington, Canada, and South Africa. By 1954 there were Religious Science and Science of Mind churches sprouting all over the landscape, as various graduates set up their own centers for the teaching. Some affiliated with headquarters, some didn't. The first church to use the name

"First Church of Religious Science"* was Carmelita Trowbridge's Alhambra chapter. Fred Bailes had termed his own chapter "The Science of Mind Church."

However, technical aspects and legal tangles were matters that Ernest delegated to others. For example, he had favored letting the ministerial association form its own group and run its own business. He suggested that he be a permanent member of the association's council, with the Institute training the leaders.

When the International Association of Religious Science Churches had been chartered, Ernest recommended that the Institute Board and the International "exchange" one member each, so that both organizations could be kept informed at their top levels. Ernest asked me to exchange places with one member of the IARSC Council, and I agreed to be the Board representative on their governing body. Evidently the director of our Field Department had been in better contact with the field leaders than Ernest had been. These included such strong personalities as Robert Bitzer in Hollywood; John Hefferlin in Long Beach; Jack Addington in San Diego; Carleton Whitehead in Monterey; Laura Holman in Glendale; and Raymond Charles Barker in New York. And each, along with others, would take his church away from affiliation with the Institute.

From the outset of the International Association's history, there seemed to be clashes of personality, resulting in friction between Ernest and some others. I would not attribute it at this late date to any resentment of Ernest's insistence on tight con-

---

*"First" in church names denotes precedence (in order of founding) only within a given locality—in this case, Alhambra, Calif.

trol. The sudden turbulence, crystallizing at the January 1954 meeting, was something foreign to my experience, and I could not comprehend at the time why the International wanted full Institute authority to license ministers and practitioners. This was certainly at complete variance with Ernest's entire concept, and he walked out on it. I had no choice but to follow.

Science of Mind magazine, which only a few months earlier had listed 58 churches, showed 16 fewer in the October 1954 issue. Half of these later returned to the fold.

Certainly some reorganization had been in order, as at one time that year we had corporate entities in two churches, an association of churches, and an Institute. Ernest and I often worked far into the night with Attorney John Huntzinger of the Board of Trustees to straighten matters out. It was not until 1955 that the details could be untangled, permitting the Church of Religious Science to come fully into being, with Ernest Holmes, its founder, rightfully in the First Chair.

Ernest felt that the means of carrying on the teaching were now in place and that the time had arrived in his life for doing other things. Having reorganized the Institute and also reorganized his own thinking, he was now ready to reorganize Ernest Holmes. In June of 1956 he turned his Beverly Hills congregation over to his assistant minister, Gene Emmet Clark, with his blessing. After thirty-seven years on the lecture platform, he told me, "I'm ready for some new experiences, like spending more time with Hazel."

The previous several years had been very hectic. Ernest's radio audience, originally with KMTC, Beverly Hills (October 6, 1933), had grown. His book *This Thing Called Life* was freely distributed by the thousands in paperback to American soldiers worldwide. In 1945, in recognition of his authorship of this book, Ernest was awarded the honorary degree of Doctor of Philosophy by India's famed Andhra Research University.

Among several other honorary degrees bestowed on him in recognition of his writings and his work were an L.H.D. in 1945 from what is now the California College of Medicine of the University of California and a Litt.D. in 1949 from the Foundation Academic University of Spiritual Understanding, in Venice, Italy.

Even earlier—in 1942—he had been named Commander of the Cross by the Association of the Humanitarian Grand Prix of Belgium, and in 1944 he was named an honorary member of the Eugene Field Society, a national group of authors and journalists. In all, over twenty honorary degrees and awards were bestowed on Ernest, so that the self-taught individual no longer had to look with envy at his brother's Phi Beta Kappa key. He had amassed more awards than his already distinguished brothers and relatives combined.

In 1949 his radio program—by then also titled *This Thing Called Life*—was syndicated nationally and aired at 4:00 P.M. each Sunday on the Mutual network. The following December, he turned it over to another speaker. When, in 1950, the United States became involved in war in Korea, *This Thing Called Life* was the only program of religious content carried on the Armed Forces radio network. The program went on long afterwards to be a continuing inspiration to many in times of stress and duress. I can still hear his opening words: "There is a Power for Good in the Universe greater than you are, and you can use It."

One of the things that Ernest wanted to explore in 1956 when leaving Beverly Hills was television. Many in the Beverly Hills congregation were creative people in the cinematic arts, and several of them were television performers. That year a special bequest made possible a half-hour TV program, also called *This Thing Called Life*, with Ernest Holmes visible once a week as well as audible. For the greater part of each half-hour he was alone in front of the camera.

Filming the television program that summer was a new experience for Ernest, and he found that he missed the audience and the live rapport. The thirteen-week series did a single re-run, making a total of twenty-six weeks that Fall. However, we found the television time frightfully expensive.

The fledgling Church was beset with every organizational problem Ernest's consciousness had anticipated, from prima-donna ministers to orthodox ("Old Thought") laymen in positions of authority. Instead of tapering off, he actually lectured more—shoring up a minister here, bolstering a faltering congregation there, starting up a new work someplace else. Ernest Holmes' world at that time was a busy one. But on the night of May 21, 1957, this world was shaken: Hazel passed away.

Ernest and Hazel: a strong duo—a team, really—now sundered. When Ernest had decided on what he thought would be semi-retirement in 1956, Hazel gave up her practitioner's office at the Institute and continued her practice in the privacy of her home.

123

She never had any interest in public speaking; indeed, I don't even recall ever hearing her speak out on any subject. She left the speaking to Ernest and discreetly stayed in the background as his conscience and confidante.

She herself had a fine clientele of professional people, with regular office hours. Both she and Ernest loved creative people—regarded them as a different breed—and it was Hazel that had brought the movie people into the work; in fact, not a few of the Hollywood movie colony were students, clients, friends, and acquaintances of Ernest and Hazel Holmes.

There was the Academy-Award-winning producer Cecil B. DeMille, long remembered for his epic religious productions *The Ten Commandments* (1923 and 1956), *King of Kings* (1957), and *Samson and Delilah* (1949). Mickey Rooney would bring each of his successive wives and children to, as he put it, "dig" the philosophy. Singer Peggy Lee was a frequent guest at the Holmeses' parties. In fact it was said that wherever two or more show-business people were gathered together in the Holmes name, there was *always* a party. Peggy would never go on a big assignment—Vegas or the networks—without Ernest's treatment work.

Together Ernest and Hazel would attend many Hollywood openings. But now came a closing—and Ernest was not quite prepared for it. Few are.

Ernest came home that night from a lecture. It was Lena the maid's night off, and Hazel always left lights on for him. Turning the lights on downstairs, he noticed that the only light was coming from an upstairs bathroom. He hurried up the stairs, entered the bathroom, and found Hazel on the floor. It had apparently been a sudden heart attack, in which she had experienced no suffering. But Ernest's shock was tremendous.

For months after her passing I would meet him in the hallway at home, pacing up and down, saying, "This is terrible. Just terrible." He depended so much on Hazel.

I'd put my arms around him and try to console him. I said, "You *know* everything is going to work out all right. You went through it with me some time ago and you know it all works out." Even though I was younger when I had lost my wife than he was now, he had managed to console and comfort me. He had, of course, treated for me, and I now did the same for him.

But the teatment is not effective unless the patient accepts it. And this was just something he could not accept—that Hazel had passed to a new experience.

Ernest depended on me more and more as he had less and less to do with the new Church during this trying period. Barclay Johnson, Mark Carpenter, and George Bendall, all of them ministers, were also stabilizing influences with Ernest during these days. The ripples of change from metaphysical Institute to metaphysical Church were rocking the ship of Church. The need for a "united" Church was plainly obvious to me, while Ernest at that point in his experience was plainly unaware of the Church's need. Finally, though, and with Ernest's blessing, the United Church of Religious Science was chartered on the sixth day of November, 1957. Still, it would be another decade before its ratification.

That was not for Ernest to see.

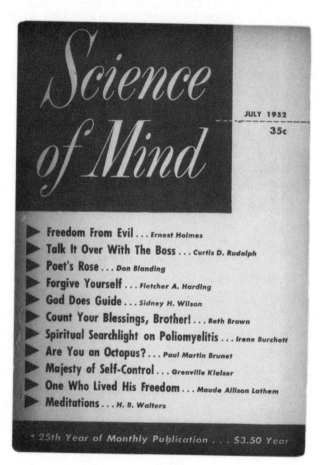

Science of Mind

JULY 1952

35c

• 25th Year of Monthly Publication ... $3.50 Year

Chapter 15

◆

THE
HEALING

ERNEST HOLMES told it like it is—always! "We are trying to organize around an idea—not a person, not a revelation, but a spiritual idea."

His idea was to create a new world movement with some definite form. He was always cautious of the intrusion of organization on his own personal independence. In accepting the format of church, he limited himself to a $10,000 annual salary and refused to hold title to property that the public paid for.

In a letter dated October 22, 1943, to Clifford L. Chaffee, a good friend and confidant of his, he states:

When we found it necessary to have branches, we found it equally necessary to so organize the work with enough authority to make it impossible for the branches to institute a teaching entirely separate and different from ours. It has been necessary not only to create a system of thought which we feel keeps faith with the best conclusions of the ages. It has become equally necessary to so organize our effort that it shall not be used for personal power, advantage or gain. It has taken me several years to come to the conclusion of the necessity for doing this.

I see no reason why we should not be able to work out our organized effort in a democratic way. We are both a school and a spiritual institution. It will be necessary for us to separate the idea of school and training from the idea of local organization. We ought to be able to work out such a federated plan and have vision great enough to maintain a spiritual democracy within the larger framework, within a unified and intelligent effort.

Because of certain thought patterns in your previous experience and in my own, . . . we both have been reluctant to do this. But now, for the sake of the greater good, I feel we should combine—we should unite.

Some years later, Chaffee, a prominent Presbyterian layman, and his wife, Sally, became leaders in the work and set up what is now known as the La Crescenta church, in Crescenta Valley. When the idea of a church there was first discussed and Ernest himself was asked to lead the group, he said, "My friends, I will gladly share with you all that I have found to be true, but I would never be your leader: because if you put me up high enough, you'll see my feet of clay."

How like Ernest to believe that all idols have feet of clay! More likely, they would have found Ernest's feet shod with low-heeled loafers, for he did enjoy his personal comfort. Hazel often had to remind him to leave the casual shoes home. "Papa," she would say, "at a church dedication service, the black lace-up shoes go so much better with the ministerial robe."

Ernest favored well-tailored but casual clothing; and I can still see him with the loafers, green-checked slacks, a sport coat, and a brightly colored tie. If he and Hazel went out in the evening, when he came home he would remove his jacket and tie and stretch out on the bed in comfort, with feet propped up.

In his search for key people to carry the teaching worldwide, one name stands out. This is William H. D. Hornaday. Bill was the son and grandson of Methodist preachers and had done church missionary work in China, where he learned to speak the language. He absorbed more of Buddha than he taught of Christ and returned to the States to go into business.

At the recommendation of a family member, Bill Hornaday attended two Sunday lectures and was so impressed that he enrolled in the night classes.

Ernest invited the businessman-student to lunch one day and during the course of the conversation indicated he had heard of Bill's background as a preacher. Modestly, Bill insisted that his present business of educational toys (he manufactured ant-villages) was fulfilling his needs quite satisfactorily. Ernest didn't ask Bill if he wanted to go back to preaching.

After luncheon, they walked back to the parking lot. As Bill got in his car, Ernest said, "Bill, I think you ought to know I've been treating because I need a preacher. My Sunday service has been standing-room-only for so long I had to start off one of our teachers in another theatre. He's had a better offer in another church and he's leaving. A *preacher*, teaching Science of Mind, could fill that theatre.''

Ernest admitted that the Belmont Theatre seated 1600 and that attendance was not anywhere near what it could be. He said, ''The man who's leaving is very able, one of our best, but—he just isn't a *preacher*; and that's what they seem to want. I'm finally convinced that you can't educate these people away from preaching. They're trying to get me to go that route— singing hymns, putting on a robe—the same old rigmarole I worked so hard to get rid of.

''A sense of humor would be an insupportable handicap to many preachers,'' Ernest continued, ''but—since I've been treating on this need for a preacher-teacher—it's only fair to tell you that the first time I heard you laugh, I felt *this could be the man*!'' Bill Hornaday did have a sense of humor and stage presence; and three generations of ministry get into a fellow's blood.

Several months later, Bill had been unable to find anybody with enough knowledge of ants—and enough money and guts —to take over his business, so he just put the whole thing in storage and showed up one Sunday at the Belmont to observe the service. He felt very uneasy in that vast auditorium with its congregation of about a hundred people. It was the present speaker's final Sunday before moving on to his new situation, and the Board of Trustees, looking at the physical record, didn't give Bill a vote of confidence.

Having treated for a minister for the Belmont, Ernest now treated for his new minister's success, then added to Bill, "Now go and prove the Principle." Afterward, he said to me, "I want you to go and help him all the way."

With Ernest it was my custom to give a 15-minute lesson and then a 5-minute treatment before the typical service. Then I would leave the thing. I saw no reason to change it for Bill—and I did treat for him. But wouldn't you know? Just as he faced the audience and they dimmed the lights of the theatre, the podium lights went out and his notes vanished in the gloom. Gone was the lecture.

He preached a *sermon*.

All the weeks of association with Ernest and the practitioners and the teachers at the Institute came out in his words—the tales told by his fellow-students, the healings he had witnessed with his own eyes, the happiness of the people resulting in eagerness. Once he got over the opening jitters, it came on just beautifully.

When we greeted the congregation at the door after the service, I overheard the head usher mention the amount of the morning offering—which was a far cry from the six thousand dollars Bill needed to keep the work in operation.

The next week, Bill told Ernest, "I'm going to announce that we need that six thousand dollars—just announce it and leave it there. I'll speak the word."

Ernest replied, "Say it once and let it go to work. That's what I always do."

Word had spread rapidly of Reverend Bill's folksy stories, and when he stepped out from the wings on that second Sunday, he beheld nearly five times the number of people he had had that first Sunday. I believe he had a bigger case of jitters than he had when he started. He kept his own counsel; but I could feel him trembling inwardly.

At the offertory, he solidly affirmed that the six thousand dollars needed to continue the basic operation at the Belmont was now forthcoming. A woman, emerging from the auditorium as we stood at the door, mentioned something about her husband, who had attended the first Sunday and was ill today. She asked Reverend Bill to treat for him, and I heard him agree to do so. Just then my attention was diverted by another conversation.

When I looked back at Bill, I thought he had been struck by lightning. The woman had gone away with a lilt in her voice, and Bill had demonstrated his six thousand dollars—an instant reaction to affirmation, proven by her check in his hand.

Bill was still shaking the next day at headquarters—but Hazel was unsurprised. "After all," she said, "Papa had confidence in you." And Ernest would later repose this confidence in Bill as his minister for Founder's Church—the preacher who was to carry on the Institute work in church form.

I'm sure my years with Ernest were a stabilizing influence to Bill each Sunday as the audience grew closer to the capacity point and he would look out over that vast sea of faces with butterflies in his stomach. And just as I was a steadying influence for Bill Hornaday, so was Bill Hornaday a steadying influence for Ernest during the year that Founder's Church of Religious Science came into being. Some of Bill's most eloquent preaching was done not from the platform or the pulpit but on a person-to-person basis with Ernest, with me, with the Board, and with individual congregational members, friends, and patrons.

To say that Bill Hornaday went out and single-handedly raised the funds that built Founder's Church would not be accurate. But to say that he talked it up from 1952 to 1958, his missionary zeal finally convincing Ernest that the church building should be built at all, would not be too far from the truth.

Hazel had said it: ''Papa had confidence in picking his heir-apparent''; and the consciousness of William H. D. Hornaday justified that confidence. His good humor, enthusiasm, and missionary ardor had us calling Bill's congregation ''Founder's Church'' long before the building bearing that name came into being. There's no doubt that Rev. Bill, later Dr. Bill, was a healing influence on the movement during those years.

Where Ernest had no particular interest in leaving the confines of the Western Hemisphere, Dr. Bill traveled extensively throughout the world, speaking to university students in Asia, Latin America, and Europe. He had been on the debating team at Whittier College in California and personally knew fellow-student Richard Nixon, who once, as student advocate, got Bill and some others out of a scrape with the college administration over a prank played against a rival campus.

Over the years, Dr. Hornaday would be invited to become Guest Chaplain to the United States Senate; receive the Award of Merit from the City of Los Angeles in recognition of his work with juvenile delinquents; receive the Armed Forces Radio & TV Service Award; be honored by the State of California in commendation of his many years of outstanding service to mankind; receive the Freedom Foundations Award; chair the Multiple Sclerosis Fund; serve on the California Advisory Commission on Civil Rights; and attend the White House Conference on Health at the invitation of President Johnson. He would also study with Dr. Carl Jung in Zurich and become acquainted with the "Reverence for Life" philosophy of Dr. Albert Schweitzer as his guest at Lambaréné in French Equatorial West Africa.

Many of these things Ernest lived to see. Naturally, they reflected creditably both on Dr. Bill and on the stature that the Church of Religious Science was achieving in the land of its birth. Meanwhile, Bill moved ever closer to Ernest during those years, not only spiritually but physically. From the Belmont he moved the Sunday service to the Uptown and then finally back to the Wiltern we had left years before.

The Wiltern crowds brought with them a kind of ongoing debate. After Sunday service, we would all go to Ernest's home, and over, perhaps, a pot of beans or some custard or something else he had cooked, the day would be discussed. Lena, the maid, always did the preparation, but Ernest insisted on supervising it. The white German Shepherd dog, Prince, was always much in evidence, for both Hazel and Ernest loved him dearly.

Ernest had had a discussion that day with some woman about junior church. The term carried Ernest's memory back over many years, for it had originated in Fenwicke's little Congregational church in Venice when "Happy" Holmes, the playground director, also helped conduct the junior church.

Since Ernest and Hazel themselves had had no children, it

was quite an admission for Ernest to realize that perhaps the need for junior church was dependent on more than theatre buildings. It reopened anew his discussion of an ''edit-fice'' (edifice), as he called it. He would never call the building a church; it was always an ''edit-fice.''

One reason the edifice had not been built was the growth of the city. People and buildings had proliferated, with especially dense growth all around the Institute property, and now there was much talk of high-rise buildings in the postwar boom. An offer to sell the adjoining corner was placed on the table at a Board meeting. All eyes went to Dean Holmes. Never really enthusiastic about a church edifice anyway, he shrugged his shoulders, and they sold the corner for $40,000.

On this Sunday, Ernest asked Bill how much it would cost to buy it back. Bill knew to the penny: $160,000. Ernest was what his long-time friend Thornton Kinney referred to as a single-entry bookkeeper. He liked to do business on the cash basis rather than on the accrual or double-entry method.

He went back to the kitchen, opened the oven door, and stirred some beans. He wouldn't permit a mortgage on his own property. ''I'll think about it,'' he said. But he was *already* thinking, and his thoughts were of Hazel—now gone.

Hazel had been an artist in her own right; and she had loved good music. He was seeing an artistically rendered edifice. ''And there must be an organ, a beautiful organ, a magnificent instrument.''

Bill Hornaday caught the vision. ''The Hazel Holmes Memorial Organ,'' he said and waited.

That clinched it.

135

Many details had to be worked out—but Ernest took an active part in the planning. He was rejuvenated, renewed, and there was the old twinkle in his eyes. "The sanctuary first," he said, "and underlying it all, the healing consciousness; and then my original dream complete: a world headquarters. And on the same theme, a teaching and publishing center."

Ernest wanted a *different* kind of church; this I know. From the day the first spadeful of earth was turned for Founder's Church of Religious Science at Sixth and Berendo streets in Los Angeles, Ernest's interest was heightened.

As the walls of the great circular auditorium started taking form, he took an increasingly active interest in the planning of the furnishings and the finishings. The plush theatre-type seats are reminiscent of the years that the church spent in the theatres of Los Angeles. The lighting and sound systems were the most modern that any theatre could possibly have. In place of a stained-glass church window, there is an immense translucent illuminated mural symbolizing the whole spectrum of human knowledge and spiritual understanding. It fills the entire wall behind the pulpit and is a strikingly beautiful work of art.

And, as promised, there is the magnificent Hazel Holmes Memorial Organ—typically, not a church organ but a *theatre* organ. Appropriately, it was at Founders, and with this organ playing, that the funeral of Jesse Crawford—"the Poet of the Organ" and America's most popular organist—was held.

The final cost of Founder's was over $1.5 million. Founder's Church today houses one of the largest metaphysical congregations in the world. Downstairs, under the sanctuary-in-the-round, are two places worthy of note.

One is a beautiful, intimate chapel done completely in white with heavy carpeting and soundproofing. The silence is something that one can feel as one enters—for it is a silence that exudes vibrations of peace and healing. It is here that the practitioners maintain a vigil for world peace every day at noon, Los Angeles time. This chapel was designed to be a memorial to Ernest Holmes—the man who would permit no memorial in his day.

The other room of interest is a place of fellowship, called Hornaday Hall—which returns us to the person who was the "prime mover" of Founder's Church. Ernest had thrown the mantle of succession onto Bill Hornaday, because the people wanted a preacher. And Bill had caught the spirit and the vision, demonstrated the philosophy—and got his church.

The demonstration was made when Founder's Church was dedicated on January 3, 1960. Next, the United Church charter, which I had kept alive over five years, was activated on the first of June, 1963, and ratified by the Convention of the United Church of Religious Science on January 6, 1967. The healing, thirteen years in coming, was now complete.

That was Ernest's great wish.

SCIENCE
OF MIND
Discussion
PROGRAM

GENERAL SUBJECT: The World We Live In

Topic—*The World We Live In*

1ST
DISCUSSION
OUTLINE
—
First Year

Chapter 16

♦

"TRY
OUT
THE
TEACHING"

THE LAST time I saw Ernest he said, "Tell Bill I don't want any fancy eulogy. Just tell the people I'm sorry I couldn't attend service because I was just too busy wherever I am." Busy practicing what he preached. I can feel his presence now, saying to all who read this book, "Try out the teaching. I know it works in your day and mine. Try out the teaching."

"His" day—now receding. Early in that life, as a teenager, he had read an essay. Inspired, he had cured himself of a cold. The essay was written by an American, Ralph Waldo Emerson. It was titled, "Self-Reliance."

Emerson predicted that a new faith would arise from out of the heartland of America. He predicted a new religion—a new concept of church.

The Mormon Church originated in America. These people believe themselves descended from the Lost Tribes of Israel. The

Christian Science religion originated in America. These people deny the reality of matter.

The missionary outreach of both Islam and Christianity has frequently been carried out with force, coercion, and the sword. Coercion and manipulation of the economic system have been the record of the religion-like zealotry of socialism and communism—a basic duality of speaking one way and acting another.

Rosicrucian writings, claiming descent from medieval alchemy and the Magi of old, have made a prediction:

> The central doctrine of religion in the future will be that of a Universal Creative Intelligence (Mind), everywhere present, impersonal, united with man not alone in a faith in the brotherhood of man, but a Brotherhood of BE-ING. There will be no sects but degrees and grades of comprehension whence each advances as he proves his competence (right of consciousness). There will not be churches but A CHURCH.

The Church of Religious Science comes closest to fulfilling this prediction of modern humanity. If today people feel cut off from God, guess who moved? As the modern person becomes aware of the truth of his or her beingness—stripped of superstition, fear, dogma, creed, convention, and orthodoxy—he becomes aware that he *is*. He or she can say, "I am," and back comes an echo from the Great I AM. Another way of saying this is, "There is One Mind; that Mind is God [Good, Allah, Krishna, Jehovah, or whatever you want to call It]; that Mind

140

is perfect; that Mind is my mind right now." That way of saying it was Ernest Holmes'.

I recall well one of Ernest's favorite sayings: "Some day we are
going to really try out the teaching of Jesus and practice Christianity." Yes, we do practice the teaching of Jesus; and no, we
are not a Christian church. As Ernest put it:

> Jesus was a man who became the Christ through his un-
> derstanding of his complete oneness with God. Through
> this understanding he made direct contact and had made
> available to him this wonderful teaching that is a model
> for all people living in any age. I don't give a damn
> whether the man ever actually lived or not. I realize that
> *somebody* said these things for recorded history. If that's
> heretical from the standpoint of orthodoxy, so be it.

We do not regard Jesus the Christ as the great exception to
life or to the natural order of things. We regard him as the great
example—the example of the ultimate way all should live.

The Science of Mind teaching is not a new religion. It is probably the oldest religion there ever was. Yet Ernest Holmes, the
little man with the big voice, cast a long, long shadow ahead
into the corridors of time. His teachings say that if the demonstration you get is fuzzy and incomplete, then the idea you
projected into subjective mind was fuzzy and incomplete to begin with.

Pioneer practitioner Ivy Crane Shelhamer, in an early issue of *Science of Mind* magazine, said:

> Given definite intention, subjective mind will work, by the Law of Growth, on a perfect outward manifestation unless it receives from the one commanding it a countermand in the form of doubt, suspense, or fear. The attitude of Unseen Power toward man is in exact proportion to his attitude toward It. The Power will recognize him as he recognizes It and will become to him in exact proportion to his acknowledgment.

Yes, this science that we are teaching is practical. It can be applied. It can be lived every day, twenty-four hours a day. The science of man and the Science of Mind are not in conflict. They never were. There can be no incompatibility, because all is natural law; all is according to the ways of nature. The universe can be nothing but the physical revelation of the Mind of God. This must have been what the apostle Paul meant when he told his people, "Let the Mind that was in Christ Jesus be in you."

One Mind—not many minds. One Church Universal, where each can learn the truth of his or her being—his oneness with the All-Good—and where each can feel that his or her own tradition, and the revelations from whatever source, are respected and making a contribution to the whole—a contribution to the constant evolvement of humankind from the depths of superstition and ignorance and fear to standing illumined in the light of its own consciousness, with peace and love in each heart—for oneself and for all others. This is in effect Ernest Holmes' synthesis. As such, it is Ernest Holmes' contribution to the progress of humankind.

As Ernest said: "Try out the teaching." This is a Space Age religion and a way of life. You are already a religious scientist, whether you realized it or not before this moment.

Now try out the teaching.

It was Ernest's, and it can be yours.